TREASURES FROM ITALY'S GREAT LIBRARIES

TREASURES
FROM
ITALY'S GREAT
LIBRARIES

Edited by Lorenzo Crinelli
Text by Anna Rita Fantoni

with 228 colour illustrations

The Vendome Press

Published in the USA in 1997 by
The Vendome Press
1370 Avenue of the Americas
New York, NY 10019

Distributed in the USA and Canada by
Rizzoli International Publications
through St. Martin's Press
175 Fifth Avenue
New York, NY 10010

Library of Congress Cataloging-in-Publication Data

Crinelli, Lorenzo.
    Treasures from Italy's Great Libraries / by Lorenzo Crinelli
        p.   cm.
    ISBN: 0-86565-986-9
1. Illumination of books and manuscripts, Medieval--Catalogs.
2. Illumination of books and manuscripts, Renaissance--Catalogs.
3. Incunabula--Illustrations-Catalogs. 4. Libraries--Italy--Catalogs.
Grandi Tesori delle Biblioteche Italiane
ND2894.18C75 1997
745.6'7'07445--dc21   97-16448
                                                 CIP
            Printed and bound in Italy

CONTENTS

INTRODUCTION

THIS PUBLICATION CONTAINS a selection of reproductions of illustrated manuscripts and early printed books chosen by the editors from those found in a cross-section of the great libraries of Italy. It makes no presumption to being representative of the vast treasures that they contain, nor is it a chronological survey of the ancient art of making books. It is rather an invitation to the reader to delight in an art normally available only to the few who are able and willing to search out its joys on the shelves of institutions generally visited only by scholars and connoisseurs on very specific missions. The editors have, however, attempted to present several of the themes that inspired usually anonymous artists to embellish the text pages that they found before them: the Old and New Testaments, mythology, music, maps, treatises on health and science, and much else. Among the rarest and most important treasures in libraries are, of course, books with no illustration at all. These are not included here as they are usually of slight aesthetic interest, remarkable though they may be. The only fixed point here has been chronological; the selection starts in the early Middle Ages and ends in the late sixteenth century.

A book could be defined essentially as a support for an intellectual message; it is an object that can offer experiences in a spectrum ranging from the simple acquisition of information to the enjoyment found in contemplation of a work of art. Its binding, not under consideration here, can often be even more astonishing than what it protects, and its physical make-up has ranged from papyrus and parchment to industrially produced paper and even, perhaps, electronic impulses radiating from outer space to a computer – in years to come, this latest development may rob many of the joys of feeling, handling and admiring what is now often referred to as a 'product'. A product, one might add, whose purpose is to encapsulate mankind's highest aspirations and which provides a legacy for every generation to follow.

PAPYRUS AND PARCHMENT

The essential element of a book has always been the material which supports its text; the first materials used included papyrus and parchment, the former being extensively employed in ancient times. Papyrus was used for a long period to make books in roll form. It was made from the stems of an aquatic shrub which were cut into strips and then glued together to form single sheets; these were joined together and wound around a wooden cylinder.

Parchment manuscripts in book form may first have been made in the first century AD. This book form was called a codex, a term which had previously been used for wax tablets that were tied together by a string passed through holes in the edges. It was however only towards the third to fourth centuries that parchment became the principal material used for the preservation and diffusion of written texts.

The first task to be undertaken in making such a book was the long and laborious process of preparing parchment. First, sheep, calf or goat hides were immersed in a water and lime solution to facilitate the removal of the hair and the remainder of the flesh. The skins were then stretched on frames and rubbed with chalk to absorb any excess fat; they were then scraped again and cut to the size of sheet that was required.

If one observes the two sides of a leaf of parchment, it is easy to recognize the outer side of the animal's skin, the so-called 'hair side', characterized by its yellowish colour and by the hair follicles, which look like tiny spots; the 'flesh side' is more uniform and is whiter. Such differences were attenuated, or even overcome, when the hides of very young animals, or even split skins were used: in this way very white and thin parchment was obtained which was often used for codices of special quality.

Holes were pricked along the edges of the prepared sheets to guide the ruling of the lines: this ruling was generally executed either with a hard point, which made a furrow on one side of the leaf and a ridge on the other, with a lead stylus, or with pen and ink.

A number of sheets prepared in this way were then put together and folded to form a gathering or quire, which was now ready for writing. The work of the scribe could then begin. First he had to prepare his pen. This was generally a goose quill taken from a left wing, which made it easier for a right-handed person to hold. He would harden the point and then cut it to the required angle and sharpen it. He could now begin to copy his text. This task demanded both care and precision since the scribe had to read and copy the text as accurately as possible, without mistakes, and at the same time leave spaces for the initials and titles, which would be added at a later stage.

As each page was completed, instructions to the illuminator and rubricator were written in pale ink in the spaces which had been left blank or in the margins. Errors of transcription which the scribe himself noticed could be immediately corrected by his scraping away the offending word or phrase and rewriting the correct text in the same space. Once a whole gathering was finished, the scribe noted the first word of the next gathering (called a 'catchword') at the bottom of the last leaf, in order to help the binder to arrange the gatherings in the correct order. This was particularly necessary in cases where several scribes and/or decorators were collaborating in producing one manuscript.

THE ILLUMINATION

Once the copying was completed, decoration could be added in the spaces left blank in the manuscript. The technique for this type of ornamentation is known as 'illumination', a word which derives from the Latin verb *illuminare*, that is, to highlight elements of text or decoration.

First, the planned decoration was sketched out with a lead point, and then defined more precisely in pen. Then it was coloured; if gold was to be used, it was applied first, because special preparations had to be made: there had to be a support which was covered with a glue with a base of water and egg white; a thin gold leaf was applied to this base and the edges were then carefully trimmed before the surface was burnished to make it shine.

The various layers of colour were then applied, moving from the lightest to the darkest tones and the outlines were defined in black or brown using a pen or brush; finally white was used to highlight the figures. All the colours were of natural origin and were mostly made from earths and minerals. Before they could be used they had to be finely ground and mixed with gum arabic and sugar or other binding substances. Once the first layer of colour had been applied, the illuminator had to wait until it had dried before he could apply the next and long pauses in the work were therefore inevitable.

Originally, when the decoration consisted of simply highlighting initial letters which occupied a space of one or more lines, it would have been executed by the scribe of the text; he would draw the initial in red or some other colour so that it stood out from the rest of the text written in black ink. Pen-flourished initials, executed in red or blue ink and embellished with arabesque designs, as well as initials decorated with curvilinear or spiral motifs, could also be executed by the scribe, since their execution only required the use of a square, compass, pen and different coloured inks. It was only when decoration became more complex that the task had to be entrusted to a separate craftsman: the illuminator.

The decoration of texts changed very little in the first centuries of the Middle Ages, but there was a more pronounced development of decoration in books intended for the Christian liturgy and the pace of this development accelerated in successive centuries under the influence of Byzantine art. From the twelfth century the human figure assumed greater importance and marginalized the ornamental elements of the decoration. Just as Byzantine art exerted an influence on the decoration of manuscripts, equally in the gothic period we see decorative foliate motifs being abandoned and substituted by architectural elements directly derived from monumental gothic sculpture.

For centuries book production was concentrated in monastic *scriptoria*, but in the twelfth and thirteenth centuries centres emerged, for example at the universities, where lay professional scribes and artists worked on the production of manuscripts. Despite this, the majority of the texts which were copied continued to be of a religious nature.

FROM THE SCRIPTORIA TO PRINTING

At the beginning of the fifteenth century a substantial change in Italian book production occurred with the introduction, in Florence, of a new style of script. The new script was developed by a group of humanists who also hunted for and collected ancient manuscripts; within thirty years its use had spread throughout Italy. It appears that the Florentine humanists' 'invention' arose from the necessity for a clearer and more legible form of writing than gothic script, which however continued to be used, above all, though not exclusively, for copying religious texts. The humanists also sought to create a more pleasing aesthetic appearance for their books. The new type of writing was known to the humanists as *littera antiqua*, and it was used not only for copying codices for their personal use, but also for manuscripts that were intended for sale or ordered on commission.

The expansion of the market led to the opening of many shops of stationers (*cartolai*) who were able to commission work from professional scribes (who often signed their work, thereby leaving documentary evidence of their activity) and then have it decorated all in a short space of time.

We know much about these developments from the writing of Vespasiano da Bisticci; his shop in Florence produced hundreds of manuscripts for some of the grandest libraries of the time, and he can truly be called an entrepreneur. His shop was much frequented by the humanists and he was the first to understand the need to produce for ready sale copies of works, particularly by Greek and Latin authors, which were much sought after at the time. He was thus not only a stationer in the strict sense (that is, someone who prepared and sold parchment and paper for making manuscripts and executed bindings), but he was also a bookseller who procured and produced texts that he was asked for, both second-hand and new. Much of his work consisted in seeking out texts that were required and where necessary commissioning scribes to copy them and illuminators to decorate them. His greatest achievement was undoubtedly the production of over two hundred manuscripts on behalf of Cosimo de' Medici for the library of the Badia at Fiesole in the space of only a few months. The fact that Vespasiano was able to complete this task ensured his reputation at both a national and international level.

During the Humanist era, the revival of classical studies and the interest in ancient Greek and Latin authors led to the formation of many princely libraries. These libraries were formed in the first place from manuscripts that had been inherited or bought on the market, but they were mainly stocked with manuscripts commissioned new from scribes and booksellers. The manuscripts were not only collected for their content, but also as symbols of wealth which bore witness to the greatness of the owner and gave him a certain prestige.

As examples of this type of collection one needs only to cite the famous libraries of the Este and the Medici, in which nuclei of inherited manuscripts were augmented with splendid codices prepared on commission to make the collections as complete as possible. Other examples are the library of Federico da Montefeltro, the Duke of Urbino, which was largely created over a brief period of time on the Duke's orders, and the library of Cardinal Bessarion, a learned Greek humanist, whose exceptional collection of mainly Greek books was left to the Venetian Republic.

However, just as this enormous production of manuscripts was taking place, printing was introduced into Italy in the mid-fifteenth century by two German printers, Pannartz and Sweynheim. Between 1465 and 1473, they worked first at the Benedictine monastery of Subiaco, where they produced the first four books printed in Italy, and later in Rome.

Subsequently two other German printers, Johann and Wendelin of Speyer, and a Frenchman, Nicolaus Jenson, opened in Venice the printing presses that were to be the most active in Italy; from 1469 to 1474 they produced between them over 130 editions.

A scribe at work, from an engraving in the Historia di Milano *of Bernardino Corio, published in Milan in 1503.*

Fresco by Melozzo da Forlì in the Vatican Art Gallery.
Pope Sixtus IV is shown entrusting the Vatican Library
to its librarian, Bartolomeo Sacchi.

To begin with, in the books produced using this new technique, the work of the printer and publisher, who were often the same person, was limited to the realization of the text. The titles and initials were added by hand by rubricators and illuminators. However, since illumination was more effectively executed on parchment, in every edition approximately twenty copies would be printed on parchment destined to be decorated by professional artists, while some paper copies were embellished with drawings in ink.

In the later fifteenth century, at a time when manuscript books and printed books co-existed in parallel, the art of illumination reached its zenith, developing different characteristics in the various Italian cities where Renaissance courts were based and there were similar developments in Germany, France and Spain.

In the sixteenth century printing established its ascendancy as the dominant means of diffusing texts, and the production of illuminated manuscripts was confined to de luxe works intended for special occasions.

THE LIBRARIES

The libraries which today house the precious manuscripts and books illustrated in this volume are among the oldest and most famous in Italy. Their long histories are marked by political and social events, and reflect the very evolution of European culture.

BIBLIOTECA APOSTOLICA VATICANA, VATICAN CITY

The history of the Papal Library is closely linked to events in the history of the church itself, which led to dispersals and additions.

A decisive change in the make-up of the collection was brought about by Tommaso Parentucelli, who was elected Pope Nicholas V in 1447. He wanted the papacy to possess an exemplary library to vie with those being set up at the time at the most important Italian courts. By the time of his death in 1455, the fundamental nucleus of the Vatican Library was established; the inventory listed approximately 1,500 codices, including 807 in Latin and 357 in Greek. Nicholas V's original plan was completed by Sixtus IV, who in 1475 officially founded the Vatican Library, which was given its own premises and entrusted to the Cremonese humanist Bartolomeo Sacchi, known as Platina.

During the fifteenth century the holdings steadily increased so that at the beginning of the sixteenth century it became necessary to add further rooms to contain the collections. At the end of the sixteenth century Sixtus V commissioned an architect, Domenico Fontana, to design a new building. At the beginning of the seventeenth century, large and important collections of manuscripts were acquired: the Palatine Library from Heidelberg, the collection of Federico da Montefeltro from Urbino and the 2,000 codices collected by Queen Christina of Sweden during her stays in France and Rome. During the eighteenth century the Ottoboni and Capponi collections were acquired, and in the nineteenth century the Borgia collection was added. The Barberini and Chigi family libraries were acquired at the beginning of the twentieth century.

BIBLIOTECA CAPITOLARE, VERONA

The Biblioteca Capitolare of Verona originated in ancient times and may already have been in existence at the time of St Zeno in the fourth century, when a *scriptorium* was set up at the cathedral to produce the religious texts needed by the church; this *scriptorium* was certainly active in the sixth century and some of the codices that it produced still survive in the library.

From the eleventh to the fourteenth centuries there was a flourishing production of liturgical and musical codices for the use of the cathedral and between the fifteenth and seventeenth centuries, the library continued to be an active cultural centre frequented by famous humanists, and significantly increased its collections. New premises to house the library, which had increased in size thanks to both public and private donations, were built in the canons' cloister between 1728 and 1780. During the twentieth century the collections were reorganized, the documents were catalogued and numerous manuscripts were restored, thanks in part to the generosity of Pope Pius IX, who had formerly been the librarian of the Biblioteca Ambrosiana in Milan.

OPPOSITE: *The main room in the Biblioteca Medicea Laurenziana, built to designs by Michelangelo Buonarroti and opened to the public on 11 June 1571.*

BELOW: *An engraving from Edward Browe,* Sehr denkwürdige und sonderbare Reisen *(Nuremberg, 1686), showing several rooms in the Nationalbibliothek in Vienna.*

The collections of the Biblioteca Capitolare are particularly varied, covering a wide range of subjects: biblical, patristic, conciliar, liturgical, juridical, literary, scientific and musical. There is also a remarkable collection of incunabula and sixteenth-century printed editions, as well as 11,000 documents which are kept in the adjoining Archives annexe.

BIBLIOTECA CASANATENSE, ROME

Cardinal Girolamo Casanate (1620–1700), a cultivated churchman, is closely linked to the library that he founded, which comprised 25,000 volumes. In his will he left the library to the Dominicans of Santa Maria sopra Minerva in Rome, together with an income of 16,000 scudi for its upkeep, enlargement and day to day management (it was to be open for six hours a day).

The library building, which is thought to have been designed by Carlo Fontana, was enlarged shortly after it opened to the public, since the main room was found to be too small to hold all the books. Various rooms were added: the manuscripts were housed in the first of these, known as the 'room of Casanate' or 'of the Cardinal', and the other rooms were used to house the incunabula, engravings and music, which were removed from the main room which was used as a reading room.

During the eighteenth century the manuscript and printed sections of the library were both notably increased thanks to the efforts of the head librarians of the Biblioteca Casanatense and their assistants. Whole libraries, several of which had belonged to various religious orders, were acquired as well as individual codices. The nineteenth century was a difficult period in the history of the library, largely because of the political situation; however some manuscripts and printed music were acquired.

As a result of the suppression of religious orders and the confiscation of their property in 1873, a controversy arose between the Dominicans and the Italian government, which was settled in 1888 with the definitive transformation of the Biblioteca Casanatense into a public state library. From that date, the collections of the Biblioteca Casanatense, which had covered all fields of knowledge, became specialized in certain disciplines: the history of religion, theology, the history of the church, Roman law, Roman history and the theatre.

BIBLIOTECA CENTRALE
DELLA REGIONE SICILIANA, PALERMO

The original nucleus of the collections of the Biblioteca Centrale della Regione Siciliana was the library set up in 1682 for the Society of Jesus, which consisted principally of works on law, theology and science. Less than a century later, following the expulsion of the Jesuits in 1767 and under an act passed on 20 June 1778 by Ferdinand I Bourbon (formerly King Ferdinand IV of Naples and Ferdinand III of Sicily), it became the Biblioteca Regia Nazionale.

Gabriele Lancellotto Castelli, Prince of Torremuzza, stands out among the various members of the 'Deputazione agli Studi' (Study Department), which organized and ran the library. He can be considered the true founder of the Royal Library, which was inaugurated on 5 November 1782. Castelli added his private library, which consisted in the main of historical and numismatic texts, to the original collections of the Jesuits from Palermo and Val da Mazzara.

From 1805 to 1860 the library was once again in the hands of the Jesuits who compiled the first general catalogue of the manuscripts as well as several special catalogues, such as that of the rare editions. On the unification of Italy, the library was finally taken away from the Jesuits to become the Biblioteca Nazionale; in 1868 it contained 70,000 volumes from eighteen monastic libraries, as well as collections donated by lawyers, scholars and politicians. In 1876 the library became the University Library, and was also given the title of National Library. It was known by this title until 1977, when it became the Biblioteca Centrale della Regione Siciliana.

BIBLIOTECA CLASSENSE, RAVENNA

The Biblioteca Classense in Ravenna was founded at the beginning of the sixteenth century by Camaldolese monks who fled from the unhealthy area of Classe and established one of the most important abbeys of the Camaldolese order near the hospital of Santa Maria della Misericordia.

Portrayal of the monk Eadwine from a manuscript of circa 1150 in Trinity College, Cambridge. The inscription framing the miniature describes him as the 'prince' of scribes.

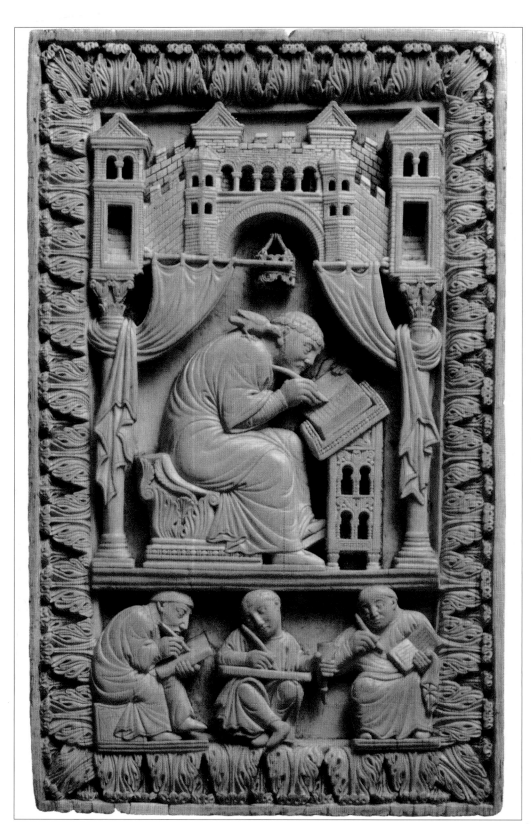

Carolingian ivory relief (960–980) in the Kunsthistorisches Museum in Vienna, representing St Gregory in the act of writing. Three monks are also shown writing in the lower margin.

The library developed significantly at the beginning of the eighteenth century under Abbot Pietro Canneti, who enriched it with codices and printed editions, which were housed in a specially constructed room. Many private and monastic libraries were added to the original nucleus in the eighteenth century, and as a result the premises had to be enlarged. In the twentieth century the Biblioteca Classense became the property of the city, and its collections were again markedly increased. Today the Classense can be described as a general library which is particularly strong in history and literature. It is also the copyright library for the province.

BIBLIOTECA ESTENSE E UNIVERSITARIA, MODENA

The collection originated as the private library of the Este family which was only open to members of the family and to the scholars and humanists who revolved around the court. In 1436 it contained 278 codices; thirty years later this number had increased to 436. The original

The main room in the Biblioteca Medicea Laurenziana in an eighteenth-century engraving by Bartolozzi-Zocchi. The manuscripts, ordered by subject, are chained to the eighty-eight tables aligned along the walls.

nucleus was collected by Leonello and his brother Borso, who welcomed important contemporary artists such as Pisanello, Andrea Mantegna and Piero della Francesca to the Ferrarese court and commissioned numerous illuminators to work on splendid manuscripts for them. The successive generations of Este dukes continued to add to the collection, but a large number of books were lost in the many fires which broke out in the archives at Ferrara, where the library was housed.

At the end of the sixteenth century Cesare d'Este was forced to cede the city of Ferrara to the Vatican State, and so the court, together with the library and archives, moved to Modena, the new seat of the dukedom. Only in the mid-eighteenth century was the library arranged and catalogued under Duke Francesco III; it was opened to the public in 1764 and at this time large sums of money were spent on acquiring not only individual books but also whole collections. In the nineteenth century, 329 particularly beautiful and rare codices came to the library from the heirs of Tommaso Obizzi del Catajo, and a fine group of incunabula and sixteenth-century printed books were also acquired, largely thanks to the efforts of Duke Francesco IV.

During the last thirty years of the nineteenth century, the library underwent significant changes. The first and foremost of these was the move to the Palazzo dei Musei, which was enforced by the municipality of Modena to make room for the Military School; this move resulted in the collection being merged with the Biblioteca Universitaria, which had been founded in 1772 by Francesco III.

The library now holds almost 4,000 manuscripts, 1,663 incunabula, over 18,000 sixteenth-century printed books, the famous music collection with approximately 2,600 manuscripts dating from the fifteenth to the nineteenth centuries, 1,600 printed musical works, 700 editions of works on musical theory and 2,500 librettos.

BIBLIOTECA MEDICEA LAURENZIANA, FLORENCE

The first nucleus of the library was formed by Cosimo de' Medici, who from his youth had studied and supported the search for manuscripts of the Greek and Latin classics. His sons, Giovanni and Piero, were also passionate collectors, but it was Piero's son, Lorenzo 'il Magnifico', who gave a notable impulse to the formation of the family library by buying Greek manuscripts in the East, with the help of the humanist and scholar Janus Lascaris. By the time of Lorenzo's death, the Medici Private Library (as it was called to distinguish it from the Medici Public Library at the Dominican convent of San Marco) contained 1,019 codices. The collection was transferred to Rome by Giovanni de' Medici (Pope Leo X), and then brought back to Florence by Clement VII, who commissioned Michelangelo to design a building worthy of the library in the cloisters of San Lorenzo.

The construction of the magnificent gallery and vestibule took many years and was only completed under Grand Duke Cosimo I de' Medici, who furnished the room with eighty-eight desks, and commissioned the wooden ceiling carved in intaglio and the red and white terracotta mosaic floor. On 11 June 1572 the library, containing approximately 3,000 manuscripts, was opened to the public.

In successive centuries the collections were enriched with manuscripts left by various Florentine families, and Count Angelo Maria d'Elci donated a valuable printed collection of Greek and Latin classics, for which a tribune was built next to Michelangelo's room. The last great acquisitions were the library of Lord Ashburnham from England and, at the beginning of the twentieth century, two thousand Greek-Egyptian papyri found during excavations made in Egypt by the Italian Papyrological Society.

BIBLIOTECA NAZIONALE CENTRALE, FLORENCE

The original nucleus of the library consists of the private collection of Antonio Magliabechi (1633–1714), which he left to the city of Florence. Numerous collections were subsequently added. The library opened to the public in 1747; in 1861 it became the Biblioteca Nazionale, and in 1885 it was renamed the Biblioteca Nazionale Centrale. Since 1870 the library has been a copyright library for all books printed in Italy. Among the most important collections which have come to the library is the Biblioteca Palatina, which includes 90,000 volumes and 3,000 manuscripts.

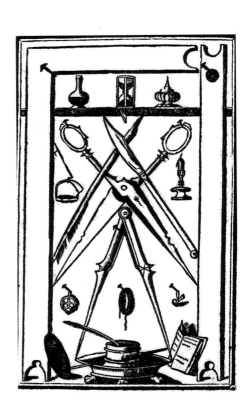

ABOVE: *An engraving from G. Antonio Tagliente,* La vera arte de lo excellente scrivere *(Venice, 1539), representing the various implements used by scribes.*

RIGHT: *Detail from an illuminated initial in the* Book of Kells *(eighth to ninth century) in Trinity College in Dublin.*

The library was housed in the Uffizi Palace until the beginning of the twentieth century. A new building, designed by the architect Cesare Bazzani, was inaugurated in 1935. The 1966 flood damaged many collections, particularly the collections of periodicals and newspapers and the German and French university dissertations. A restoration workshop, organized in various sectors, was set up as a result of the flood. As well as the copyright printed books, the library has an important collection of manuscripts and autographs, and rich holdings of music and prints.

BIBLIOTECA NAZIONALE MARCIANA, VENICE

The original nucleus of the Biblioteca Marciana consists of approximately one thousand codices collected by Cardinal Bessarion, who set out to save documents pertaining to Greek culture from destruction by the Turks. The codices were given by him to the Venetian Republic in 1468 and thanks to the intervention of the Procurator of St Mark, Vettor Grimani, the Doge, Andrea Gritti, and the librarian, Pietro Bembo, they were housed in the Ducal Palace until more suitable premises could be created.

The new building, significantly situated opposite the Basilica of San Marco and the Ducal Palace, was begun in 1537 to designs by Jacopo Sansovino. The vestibule, the ceiling of which is decorated with a large canvas by Titian, is reached from the entrance staircase. The walls of the main room are decorated with portraits of philosophers and there are twenty-one tondos on the ceiling executed by Mannerist artists who worked for the Grimani family.

Neighbouring rooms, which were once occupied by the procurator's offices, were adapted for the use of the library in the Napoleonic era. The Mint, built by Sansovino between 1537 and 1547, once housed the offices of the Republic where money was coined; the original courtyard of this building, now glassed in, has been adapted as a reading room since 1904.

In the seventeenth and eighteenth centuries, numerous codices and printed books bequeathed by noblemen and scholars, as well as volumes from the libraries of suppressed religious corporations, were added to the collection of Bessarion. The library also has an important collection of music and of geographical manuscripts, as well as a map made in the mid-fifteenth century by the Camaldolese cartographer, Fra Mauro.

BIBLIOTECA NAZIONALE VITTORIO EMANUELE III, NAPLES

The setting up of a public library in Naples formed part of the programme of reforms of Carlo di Borbone, which was only carried out by his son, Ferdinando IV. To the original Farnese nucleus of the library, transferred to Naples in 1735, were added the libraries of the Jesuits and of the Accademia Ercolanese, and, following the suppression of the religious corporations, the library of the Augustinians of San Giovanni a Carbonara. During the decade of French dominion, the library was further increased by the acquisition of its oldest and most precious collections. The contents of the library were reorganized after the return of the Bourbons, and this process continued even after the library joined the public state system in 1860.

The library is housed in the Royal Palace, built in the seventeenth century to designs by Domenico Fontana. The rooms are richly frescoed and contain shelving from pre-unification public, royal and aristocratic libraries. The new premises were inaugurated on 17 May 1827 and named after Vittorio Emanuele III.

Today the contents of the Naples Library is exceptionally varied, with an emphasis on works on history, philology, archaeology, art and literature, and there is a collection of approximately 13,000 manuscripts. The collection of the Herculaneum papyrus workshop, set up for the study and conservation of more than two thousand papyri, which were brought to light during the excavations at the Villa dei Pisoni at Herculaneum between 1752 and 1754, is of particular importance.

The numerous collections of correspondence, which are important for the light they shed on the protagonists of the culture, history and politics of southern Italy, are particularly noteworthy; in the autograph collections the most notable are those of Saint Thomas Aquinas and Giacomo Leopardi. The exceptional cartographic collection consists of 4,000 items: drawings, geographic, military and hydrographic maps and a collection of seventeenth-century celestial and terraqueous globes.

BIBLIOTECA REALE, TURIN

The Biblioteca Reale was founded as a result of the financial, administrative and cultural reform program of the Kingdom of Sardinia, which was instituted by King Carlo Alberto. In the very year that he was nominated king he paid particular attention to the court library, which he rebuilt and enlarged, acquiring new works and opening it for use not only by officials and functionaries, but also by the intellectuals of Piedmont.

The small nucleus of the court library was augmented by the king's personal collections. These contained principally military works, but also included volumes on the history of the dynasty and its dominions, heraldry and graphics, which had been built up by the first librarians.

The library was, and still is, housed in the Royal Palace, built in 1646 by the Regent Christina of France. The present interior of the library was projected in 1841 by the architect,

Illuminated initial from the Worms Bible (twelfth century) in the British Library in London. On the left, the letter is shown displaying the various stages in its execution, from the preparatory drawing to the application of gold and colours. On the right, the initial is shown as it appears in the manuscript.

German engraving dated 1520 showing a manuscript workshop. The various implements of the craft can be seen on the desks at which the scribes are writing.

painter and sculptor Pelagio Palagi. He planned the large students' room, which is a long rectangle with a barrel-vaulted ceiling frescoed to resemble Neo-Classical stucco-work. Two orders of elegant glass-fronted cases run along the walls, and above there is a gallery from which the higher sections can be reached.

The Biblioteca Reale contains approximately 185,000 volumes, 4,300 manuscripts, 186 incunabula, 5,000 sixteenth-century printed books, 2,000 drawings, 1,500 charters and numerous engravings and nautical maps. The most important of the drawings are by Leonardo da Vinci, especially the codex dealing with the flight of birds, which was bought in the nineteenth century.

Following the unification of Italy, collections were acquired of the ancient statutes of the pre-unification states and numerous homages to sovereigns, consisting of photographic collections and eulogistic musical works. After the creation of the Republic, when the property of the House of Savoy passed into the hands of the state, the Biblioteca Reale became one of the Italian state libraries.

BIBLIOTECA TRIVULZIANA, MILAN

The library originated from the collections of the Trivulzio family. From the fifteenth century on, but especially during the eighteenth century, they acquired many codices which had belonged to the libraries of suppressed religious institutions, aristocratic families, and even the dukes of Milan. The library was bought at the beginning of the twentieth century by the municipality of Milan which augmented the collections by the acquisition of bibliographic repertories. In 1935 it was merged with the Biblioteca dell'Archivio Storico Civico, which was founded with the aim of illustrating the history of Milan and various aspects of its dukedom. From that year onwards, a number of private libraries were acquired, which were especially rich in their large collections of printed works.

The Biblioteca Trivulziana, which is housed in the Castello Sforzesco, owns not only a rich collection of manuscripts, but more than two thousand charters and thousands of letters and unbound documents. The library was rebuilt between 1956 and 1963, when the Castello Sforzesco was restored.

THE MANUSCRIPTS
AND EARLY PRINTED
BOOKS

OLD TESTAMENT

Naples, Biblioteca Vittorio Emanuele III

I. B. 18, FOL. 4V

T HE MANUSCRIPT IS A FRAGMENT of only eight leaves, containing part of the Old Testament, from Job 40: 8 to Proverbs 3: 19. It dates from the end of the fifth century and is written in uncials in the Coptic-Sahidic language, the dialect used in Southern Egypt from the first centuries of the Christian era.

Folio 4v of the manuscript is illustrated by a large pen drawing representing Job with his three daughters. The miniature is an important witness to the evolution of Coptic art at the time of its transition from the Hellenistic tradition to a more linear style. Although it does not appear that the execution is by a skilled hand, the artist must have had a considerable culture.

Job is shown bearded and crowned and wearing a short tunic; his daughters wear pepla and are bedecked with jewels and diadems. The iconography of Job is very different from that found in successive centuries, for from the early Middle Ages, Job, who is known only from the book in the Bible named after him, was represented either as a humble and subdued figure sitting on a dung-heap, or as a derided hero.

The manuscript belonged to the collection of Coptic-Sahidic codices of the Museo Borgiano at Velletri, which was founded by the cardinal and scholar Stefano Borgia (1731–1804); he established this famous museum in Velletri with the help of his missionary contacts. In 1821 the manuscripts from the museum were bought from Countess Adelaide Borgia by the Biblioteca Borbonica at Naples.

VIRGIL, Works
(Virgilius Romanus)

Vatican City, Biblioteca Apostolica Vaticana

VAT. LAT. 3867, FOL. 3V

THIS IS ONE OF THE OLDEST MANUSCRIPTS that contains the works of Virgil and it is of fundamental importance for the appraisal of miniature painting in the Roman period.

The manuscript originally consisted of 410 leaves, of which 309 survive, with nineteen miniatures which illustrate the beginning of each book.

In the *Eclogues* the decoration fills only a third of a leaf, but each of the books of the *Georgics* and the *Aeneid* originally began with two full-page scenes on facing pages. The loss of many leaves means that occasionally this arrangement no longer pertains, and to make matters worse the manuscript was rebound when it first entered the Vatican collections in the fifteenth century and the order of the surviving leaves was altered.

The text is in the hand of a single scribe and is copied on exceptionally fine parchment; the decoration is likewise attributed to a single artist. The style of both the script and the painting suggests that this magnificent manuscript was produced in Rome at the end of the fifth century.

The miniature on fol. 3v shows Virgil holding a roll, with a reading desk on his left and a container for rolls on his right.

PROCVLVILLARVMCVLMINATVMANT
ADVNTALTISDEMONTIBVSVMBRAE

CORYDON

CORYDONPASTORARDEBATALEXIN
NINECOVIDSPERARETHABEBAT
DENSASVMBROSACACVMINAFAGOS
EBATIBIHAECINCONDITASOLVS

DIOSCORIDES, Herbal (Naples Dioscorides)

Naples, Biblioteca Vittorio Emanuele III

VIND. GR. 1, FOLS. 23, 59, 90

THIS ANCIENT CODEX, which is imperfect at the beginning and end, is a Herbal, that is a text which deals with medicinal plants. Many such texts were inspired, although generally indirectly, by the work of Dioscorides, *De materia medica*. In this work, Dioscorides, a doctor born in Anazarbus in Cilicia in the first century AD, described all the known medicines derived from plants (he included approximately six hundred), animals and minerals. The Naples manuscript diverges from this model, for it deals only with plants. The illustrations are painted in the upper half of the recto of the leaves, with the text laid out in two or three columns in the lower half. Rather than being scientific in aspect, like the text of Dioscorides, the Naples Herbal takes the form of a manual or didactic compendium in which the plants are arranged in alphabetical order and carefully illustrated. Neither the scribe nor the artist concerned has been identified. In the eighteenth century it was thought that the manuscript had been produced in the East; however recent research has proved that it was made in the West. The type of script, the annotations, and the style of the miniatures suggest that it was produced in Italy at the beginning of the seventh century. Some scholars think that it was made in the exarchate of Ravenna, while others have related it to the circle of Cassiodorus, to high-ranking social groups or, more feasibly, to a circle of cultured Byzantine officials. If this last hypothesis is correct, it suggests that there was still a workshop producing Greek books in south-central Italy at that time.

The manuscript is also important for other reasons: it is one of the very few pre-ninth-century Greek codices to contain a non-Christian work, and furthermore, the marginal notes, which were added in the thirteenth and fourteenth centuries, reveal contact with the Medical School of Salerno.

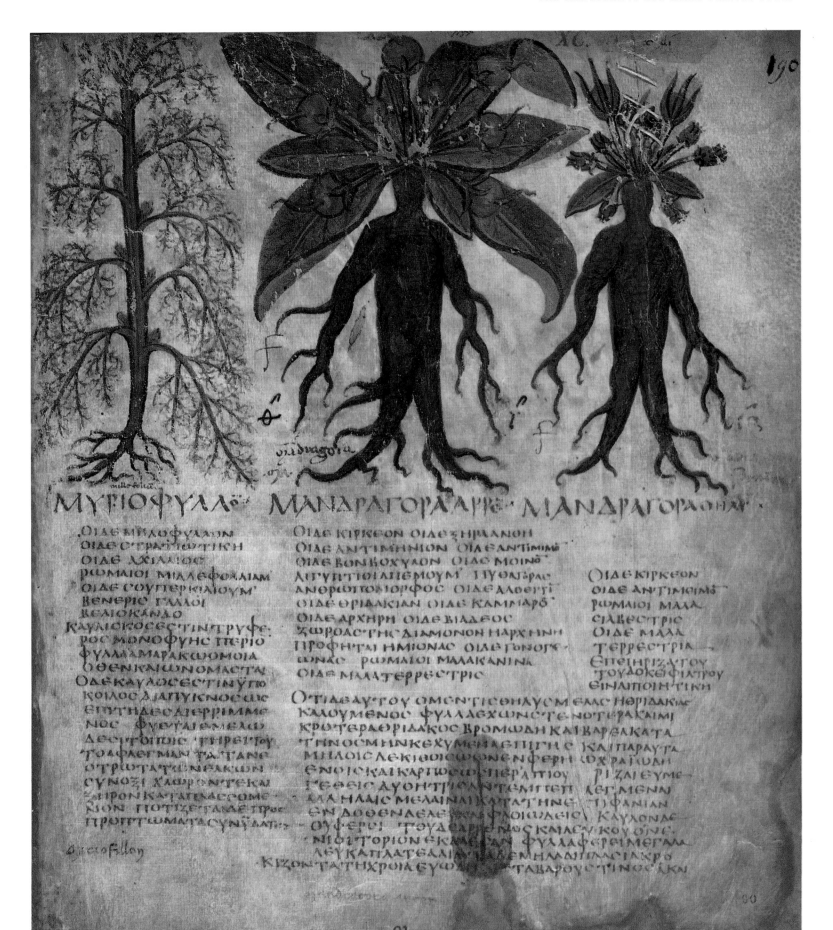

GOSPEL BOOK (The Lorsch Gospels)

Vatican City, Biblioteca Apostolica Vaticana

PAL. LAT. 50, FOL. 67V

THE IMPERIAL SCRIPTORIUM or Court School of Charlemagne produced manuscripts of great magnificence. One of these was the present codex, which is the latest example of the work of this school and one of the most famous manuscripts of the mid-ninth century.

It is the second part of a great Gospel Book, which belonged to the abbey of Saint Nazarius at Lorsch (Germany), where it remained until the fifteenth century. It was then rebound in two volumes: the first part, containing the canon tables and the Gospels according to Matthew and Mark, is now in the Batthyaneum Library at Alba Julia in Romania; the second part, containing the Gospels according to Luke and John, came into the Palatine Library in Heidelberg in the sixteenth century, and then, together with the rest of the contents of the Palatine Library, was transferred to the Vatican Library in 1622.

The original carved ivory binding is also now divided: the ivory plaque from the front board is now in the Victoria and Albert Museum in London, while the ivory from the back is conserved in the Vatican Museum.

The text, written in gold by several hands, is laid out in two columns and framed by illuminated borders; the design and colour of the borders vary on every two pages with no repetition. There are also full-page portraits of the four Evangelists; the iconography of these miniatures reflects Greco-Roman illumination, while the decorative elements of the borders reveal Insular influence.

The miniature shown here represents Saint John the Evangelist sitting on a throne beneath a great arch in the act of writing his Gospel. The richness of the decorative detail is highlighted by the abundant use of gold in his clothes and in the background curtains, as well as by the use of lapis lazuli to paint the capitals and the precious marble of the columns.

GOSPEL BOOK

Modena, Biblioteca Estense

GR. I (= α. M. 9. 5), FOL. IIV

THE MANUSCRIPT, which is datable to the end of the tenth century, contains three hundred leaves of text. There were originally miniatures showing all four Evangelists, but only three remain because the one for Luke is lost.

Fol. IIV shows Matthew, seated on a stool with a pink cushion, writing in a large book resting on his knees. Facing him is a high reading-desk with a bench below on which a book and various writing instruments are placed. Two churches are illustrated *a graffito* on the gold background. It is a miniature of the highest quality, in which drapery, beard and hair are portrayed with great refinement. The scene is surrounded by a frame decorated with small circles containing stylized flowers. Further borders with small circles, leaves and flowers decorate the openings of the actual Gospels, the titles of which are written in gold capitals.

The manuscript is one of the finest examples of the third phase (tenth–twelfth centuries) of Byzantine art. The iconography is typical of Gospel Books of this period: the Evangelists are represented on the page preceding the text, seated either in the process of writing or meditating, and set against a gold ground. The ornamentation of this period is becoming more complex with the forms tending to harmonize with the fresh and brighter colours.

The manuscript was probably bought in Venice by Duke Alfonso II d'Este in 1560; it was transferred to Vienna in 1589 by Francesco d'Este and returned to Italy under the Convention of Florence of 1868.

COLLECTION OF MEDICAL TEXTS

Florence, Biblioteca Medicea Laurenziana

PLUT. 74. 7, FOLS. 195V, 200

THE MANUSCRIPT WAS WRITTEN by the doctor Niceta between the end of the tenth and the beginning of the eleventh century, probably in the imperial *scriptorium* in the time of Constantine VII Porphyrogenitos. It is a collection of medical works by Hippocrates, Galen, Oribasius, Heliodorus, Archigenes, Antillus, Asclepiades, Diocles, Amyntas, Apollonius of Citium, Nymphodorus, Apelles, Rufus of Ephesus, Soranus of Ephesus, Paul of Aegina and Palladius. The writings of some of these authors are known to us only from this manuscript and from no other source: the most important texts are by Apollonius of Citium (first century BC), who writes on the resetting of fractured limbs – of which two examples are illustrated here – and by Soranus of Ephesus (second century AD), who discusses different forms of bandaging.

The texts are illustrated by fifty-six miniatures, thirty of which are full-page (fols. 182–223v) and illustrate the text of Apollonius, each framed by an arch supported by Corinthian capitals. Though it has Hellenistic characteristics, the iconography derives from an antique prototype which was probably not fully understood in transposition. This explains the numerous errors in the representation of surgical instruments and the decoration with arches, which is of Byzantine origin and is frequently found in the decoration of the canon tables of the concordances of the Gospels.

The manuscript belonged to the hospital adjoining the Church of the Forty Martyrs in Constantinople, where it remained until the fourteenth century. It was bought by Janus Lascaris, the learned Greek humanist who bought many Greek manuscripts for Lorenzo de' Medici 'il Magnifico' during his repeated trips to the East. Lascaris signed the contract for the purchase of this and other manuscripts in Constantinople in 1492 during his second trip; the codices arrived in Italy only after the death of Lorenzo.

PSALTER
(Heidelberg Psalter)

Vatican City, Biblioteca Apostolica Vaticana

PAL. LAT. 39, FOL. 44V

IN THE MIDDLE AGES, the Book of Psalms was considered to be the most important book in the Old Testament. This manuscript, one of twenty Psalters in the Fondo Palatino of the Vatican Library, comes from the Monastery of Saints Michael and Stephen in Heidelberg, as can be seen from a note in the necrology. It dates from the eleventh century and was written and decorated in southern Germany. Some scholars believe that it could have been produced in the monastery of Lorsch, while others, on the basis of an analysis of the calendar, consider that it was made at Bistum.

Additions datable to the late thirteenth century were made to the manuscript; these include a calendar for Worms, St Jerome's Letter 106, notes on the quadripartite Psalter and the Office of Corpus Christi. There are also annotations to the antiphons and responsories in a fifteenth-century hand. These additions suggest that this Psalter was not used just as a prayer book, but as a book for study; this theory is supported by the manuscript having marginal notes in German. The manuscript may have belonged to the Dominican nuns of Strasbourg in the fifteenth century; by 1548 it was in the hands of Count Palatine Otto Heinrich, whose motto M D Z (*Mit der Zeit*) is found on the last leaf.

The decoration consists of initials and a large miniature on fol. 44v representing David and four named musicians in front of the Ark of the Covenant, set against a purple ground. The composition is divided into two levels. In the upper register the Ark is flanked by two angels, a cherubim and a seraphim; in the lower register are the five figures playing musical instruments.

OPPIAN, Cynegetica

Venice, Biblioteca Marciana

GR. Z. 479 (= 881), FOLS. 23, 39, 59

THIS DIDACTIC POEM on the techniques of hunting with dogs was written by Oppian of Apamea in Syria. The poem is written in four books: the first and most important, preceded by a dedication to Caracalla and an invocation to Artemis, contains a description of the physical qualities of the huntsman, the equipment and weapons used and the seasons and times of day suitable for hunting. These are followed by descriptions of dogs and horses, the animals most frequently used in hunting.

The manuscript has been dated to the eleventh century on the basis of an analysis of the script and the style of the miniatures. Several lost leaves were replaced in the fifteenth century. *The Life of Oppian* by Constantine Manasses, on folios 67v–68v, was added to the manuscript in the thirteenth century.

The text is illustrated by 150 miniatures that fall into two groups. In the main group, the scenes shown are closely linked to the text and derive from a late antique model: they show hunting techniques, dogs, horses and other animals. There is also a smaller group of mythological scenes. The scenes illustrated here belong to the second group: the Banquet of Phineus (fol. 23) and the Naumachia or naval battle (fol. 39), which probably derives from a chronicle. The story of the banquet, on the other hand, is found in Apollonius Rhodius and later in Apollodorus. The blind king is represented in the centre of the scene, surrounded by harpies who hurl themselves at the table in an attempt to take away a goblet; the five Argonauts are depicted on either side and a servant offering a dish is placed in the foreground. The miniature on fol. 59 shows three fishermen using a flambeau to attract fish into their nets.

The manuscript, which once belonged to the humanist Giovanni Aurispa, came into the possession of Cardinal Bessarion, who commissioned the scribe George Tribizias to provide a copy of the missing text which had been on the lost leaves; he later donated the manuscript to the Venetian Republic.

PASSIONARY

Florence, Biblioteca Nazionale Centrale

II. I. 412, FOLS. 24V, 39

THIS MANUSCRIPT, which originally consisted of two volumes with a total of 350 leaves, contains an account of the lives of the martyrs. Over the centuries the manuscript has suffered a considerable amount of re-arrangement and dismemberment. As a result, of the 158 lives that were originally included, only eighty survive and even these are no longer arranged in the order of the calendar.

The text, written in two columns, is accompanied by eighty-five miniatures. Some pages just have simple initials decorated with foliate motifs, but on others there are illustrations of one or more saints. These follow various typologies. The human figure is shown either full or half-length, either beside the text or within the initial (as in the case of Saint Fructuosus contained in the initial 'D' on fol. 24v). There are rarer instances in which the portrait of the saint serves a purely illustrative function, both in terms of its size and the position of the figure on the page: the saint is detached from the text and indeed occupies a part of the space usually allotted to the writing. A good example is on fol. 39, where we can see the figures of Saints Faustinus and Giovita (whose feast day is on 15 February) wearing white tunics and coloured cloaks. The quality of the painting is not uniform; the decoration of the first volume of the Passionary is finer and markedly influenced by Byzantine art, while the part which originally illustrated the second volume is of inferior quality.

The content and decoration of the manuscript suggest that it was produced in central Italy, and more precisely in the region of Arezzo in southern Tuscany. Opinion is divided as to its date: some scholars believe that it was made in the second half of the eleventh century, while others date it earlier, to the first half of the century.

The Passionary belonged to the Benedictine Abbey of Saints Flora and Lucilla at Arezzo, where it remained until the end of the sixteenth century, when it passed to the church of the Badia in Florence.

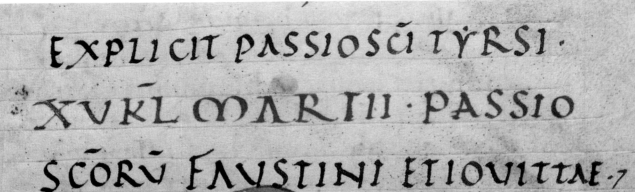

EXPLICIT PASSIO SCŪ TẎRSI·

XVKL MARTII · PASSIO

SCŌRŪ FAVSTINI ET IOVITTAE ·⁊

Faustini q

Beatissimi
uiri fau
stinus &
iouitta no
bilissimi in
ciuitate bri
xiana horti
parentibus·
fidem xp̄i
quam religiosa
mente didice
rant· instanti
sollicitudine
p̄dicabant·
Erant enim
non solum ger
manitate carnis
coniuncti· sed
eciam uirtute

sp̄s ita uniti· ut concordi ubiq; studio
xp̄m annuntiantes copiosam regionis
illius multitudinem· aduere fidei

EXULTET ROLL

Vatican City, Biblioteca Apostolica Vaticana

BARB. LAT. 592, FOL. 4

I LLUSTRATED LITURGICAL ROLLS, one of the most distinctive book forms of the Latin Middle Ages, were produced in southern Italy. Their originality is not only in their form – the roll – but above all in their extremely rich and carefully executed decoration. Many copies of the *Exultet* have survived; it was the prayer recited from the ambo by the deacon for the benediction of the candle during the Easter Vigil. The illustrations are arranged facing the opposite way from the writing so that while the celebrant reads the text the congregation could follow it through the pictures. The Vatican *Exultet* was produced in the *scriptorium* of Montecassino towards the end of the eleventh century (about 1087), when Desiderius was abbot.

The decoration, executed before the text was written, is the work of two artists. They display similar characteristics although their work is not of equal quality; in several miniatures both their hands can be identified.

The painting illustrated here represents the praise of the bees, which symbolize the virginity of Mary. The scene is divided into two clearly distinct zones: on the left two bee keepers are collecting wax from the bottom of a hive; on the right two others are inducing the migration of a swarm using smoke from a brazier.

GOSPEL BOOK

Florence, Biblioteca Medicea Laurenziana

ACQ. E DONI 91, FOLS. 30V, 96

THE TEXT OF THE GOSPELS, laid out in two columns, is preceded by two series of canon tables (fols. 1–7, 8–13). The first series is contained between arches supported by columns; the decoration is unfinished and in the main merely drawn in lead. The second series, executed in ink and in some cases not entirely finished, differs from the rest of the manuscript both in its style and in its smaller dimensions.

The Gospels are interspersed with full-page initials, portraits of the Evangelists (Matthew is shown on fol. 30v) and a painting of the Ascension (fol. 96).

The decoration of the initials (the larger ones are of finer quality than those of smaller dimensions, which are executed in a more summary fashion) has been compared to that of the Calci Bible, and it has been suggested that the two manuscripts were decorated by the same artist. The scenes with figures are more problematic: executed in the style typical of the school of Reichenau, in the past they were considered typical examples of Ottonian illumination of the beginning of the eleventh century.

Although the writing (which has been dated to the 1160s and ascribed to the neighbourhood of Pisa) and the illumination appear to be chronologically irreconcilable, codicological analysis of the manuscript has shown that they are closely linked. A solution proposed to the problem of how a twelfth-century Pisan manuscript could contain German illumination executed 150 years earlier, is that the scenes with figures were executed by an artist (probably German), who had seen a Reichenau school prototype which he used as a model. The manuscript is remarkable as an isolated example in Tuscan illumination of the twelfth century of a type which did not have any influence on contemporary artistic production.

There is no documentary evidence for the later history of this Gospel Book, as it has no later annotations. It was bought by the Biblioteca Laurenziana in 1823.

SACRAMENTARY

Florence, Biblioteca Medicea Laurenziana

CONV. SOPPR. 292, FOL. 95V

THE SACRAMENTARY CONTAINS the collection of the main prayers of the Mass, introduced by the *Vere dignum* formula. In some cases, particularly in the eleventh and twelfth centuries, the final part of this type of liturgical text became an actual Missal, concerned principally with ritual and votive masses.

The manuscript was produced in the neighbourhood of Florence in the third quarter of the twelfth century. This attribution is based on its decoration which consists of numerous illuminated initials, probably the work of a single artist, some of them simply ornamented, while others enclose figures of saints.

The only full-page miniature, on fol. 95v, consists of a mandorla containing Christ in Majesty holding the Book of the Gospels in his left hand. The scene is completed by the symbols of the four Evangelists set outside, at the four corners of the miniature. Some of the decorative details, particularly the plastic modelling of the drapery, suggest the influence of an illuminator known as 'Maestro Corbolino', in whose work a marked Byzantine influence can be detected.

The likelihood that this manuscript was produced in or near Florence is suggested not only by the style of its decoration, but also by the inclusion in it of masses for saints honoured in the diocese of Florence, such as Romolo, Reparata, Cerbone, Miniato and Frediano, and of two offices for Saint Romolo, one of which was copied in the margin in the twelfth to thirteenth century. It is therefore probable that the Sacramentary, whose presence is documented at the monastery of Camaldoli, was not originally intended for the diocese of Arezzo (saints venerated in Arezzo are not included), but was transferred there subsequently. It was kept at the monastery until 1809, when it came to the Biblioteca Laurenziana following the suppression of religious corporations by the Napoleonic government.

EIGITUR CLEMEN
TISSIME PATER

LUCAS DE GAIL, Roman de Tristan

Modena, Biblioteca Estense

EST. 59 (= α. T. 3. 11), FOLS. 48V, 79

SOME LEAVES ARE MISSING at the beginning and end of this manuscript, which dates from the thirteenth century and contains one of the various prose versions of the story of Tristan and Isolde.

The surviving decoration, in some cases badly damaged, consists of twenty-seven pen drawings set in the lower margins of the pages. They were executed by a French artist who only partially coloured the background and figures, the faces of which are characterized by a single touch of red on the cheeks. Although the subjects are somewhat uniform and the figures appear in repetitive poses, the drawing is lively and fluid.

The detail of fol. 48v shows the duel between Tristan and Palamedes: they are watched by Isolde, who looks out from a window of a building, and by two figures on the lower floor. The composition is closed on the right by an armed knight on horseback.

The drawing on fol. 79 shows the duel between Melegrant and Lamorat.

PLINY THE ELDER, Naturalis historia

Florence, Biblioteca Medicea Laurenziana

PLUT. 82. 1, FOLS. 2V-3

THE MANUSCRIPT CONTAINS the first sixteen books of Pliny's work; books 17 to 27 are in the companion volume, Plut. 82.2.

The beginning of the prologue, on fol. 2v, is decorated with a beautiful initial; the facing page shows the author on the left before the Emperor Titus. At the top of the tree separating them a small figure holds a scroll with the inscription '*Petrus de Slagosia me fecit*'; this is therefore the self-portrait and signature of the illuminator.

The codex, which dates from the thirteenth century, has a complex history. Two notes in this manuscript and its companion tell us that the Dominican friars of Lübeck had lent the two volumes to Gherardo Bueri, who was a relation of Cosimo de' Medici 'il Vecchio' (the Elder) and the head of the Lübeck branch of the Medici Bank. Documentary evidence confirms that Cosimo de' Medici, at the instigation of the humanist Niccolò Niccoli, thus succeeded in bringing this important copy of Pliny's work to Florence. In 1436 the friars asked for their books back, but evidently without success.

The manuscript came to the library of the Dominican convent of San Marco in Florence probably with Niccoli's library after his death in 1437, and may have entered the Biblioteca Laurenziana through the intervention of Grand Duke Cosimo I, before the library was opened to the public in 1571.

PSALTER

Florence, Biblioteca Medicea Laurenziana

MED. PAL. 13, FOL. 1

THIS FRENCH MANUSCRIPT CONTAINS numerous ornamental initials as well as eight which are historiated at the beginnings of the sections into which the text is divided. On fol. 1, at the beginning of the Psalm *Beatus vir*, Christ is shown in majesty in the upper part of the initial 'B'. He wears a pink garment and blue cloak, his right hand is raised and in his left he holds the terrestrial globe. In the lower part of the letter, David is playing the lyre, surrounded by other musical instruments. In the four corners of the initial, which is set in a frame decorated with geometric motifs, there are four circular medallions with scenes from David's life: these are the appearance of the angel to David, the struggle between David and Goliath, David beheading Goliath, David presenting Goliath's head to Saul.

The style of the figures and the choice of colour and ornament in the Psalter have led to comparisons with the Psalter of Albenga Cathedral. It has been suggested that the illuminator was a collaborator of the 'Albenga Master' who illuminated the Albenga Psalter. The artist, active in the first half of the thirteenth century, displays typically Parisian features; his work is characterized by a somewhat limited figure repertory, shallow folds in the drapery and a preference for red and blue tones.

On the basis of the saints invoked in the litanies, among whom appears Saint Symphorianus, martyr of Autun, it has been suggested that the codex was made for a patron from north-eastern France, between Burgundy and Champagne.

The manuscript belonged to the Lorraine family and was in the Biblioteca Palatina at the Pitti Palace, which was transferred to the Biblioteca Medicea Laurenziana in 1771.

JUSTINIAN, Corpus Iuris Civilis

Verona, Biblioteca Capitolare

CLXXIII, FOL. I

THE MANUSCRIPT, WHICH DATES from the first half of the thirteenth century, contains the *Corpus Iuris Civilis* of Justinian, Emperor of the East between
527 and 565. In the four collections of texts which form his work, Justinian brought
together the constitutions of the emperors and the texts of Roman jurisprudence.

The text is accompanied by the commentary of Accursius (1182–1258/1260), which
synthesizes almost all the commentaries by the various teachers of law on the different
parts of Justinian's collection. The commentary, which was added to the manuscript in
the fourteenth century, is arranged around the text of the *Corpus*, the leaves of which
were increased in size by the addition of strips of parchment to the lower margins so
that the commentary could be accommodated. Glosses by Odofredo Denari (1210–
1265) and Martino da Fano (1190–1272) have also been added, and in the spaces
between the lines survive the glosses by Azzo (composed at the beginning of the
twelfth century) which were erased in the margins to leave space for later commentaries.

The decoration consists of brightly-coloured illuminated initials, outlined in black,
at the beginning of each book. The initial on fol. 1 shows the Emperor Justinian
supporting the letter 'C', which is decorated with vine scrolls, volutes, and floral motifs.
In the other books, the initials are inhabited with fantastic animals, while the lesser red
and blue letters are decorated with penflourishing.

On the first page an annotation, probably a customs registration, dated 20 December 1432, shows that the manuscript was then being transferred from one town to
another, probably by a student or scholar.

The manuscript then or subsequently belonged to the Ravenna notary Francesco da
Mantova, and a note on the end flyleaf tells us that he sold it on 30 June 1459 to Paolo
Dionisi, who left it in his will to the Biblioteca Capitolare.

MEDICI ANTIPHONER

Florence, Biblioteca Medicea Laurenziana

PLUT. 29. 1, FOL. IV

THIS MANUSCRIPT, SMALL IN FORMAT (230 x 155 mm) but consisting of 411 leaves, contains twenty-seven collections of all the most important types of Latin musical texts (polyphonic chants and motets) starting from the middle of the twelfth century; it is the largest and most important collection of the musical repertory of Notre-Dame in Paris. Considering the inclusive contents of the manuscript, it is inappropriate to call it an 'antiphoner', but it was given this name long ago because of the compositions with which it begins, which are of a strictly liturgical character.

Not only are the contents important, but the decoration is also particularly fine. It consists of fourteen miniatures. The first, illustrated here, represents the classification of music according to Boethius; the other thirteen are actually historiated initials showing either Biblical scenes or scenes closely linked to the subjects which occur in the musical passages.

The codex was produced in Paris in the mid-thirteenth century in the atelier of Johannes Grusch (a famous school in Paris active from 1235 to 1270); it may have been made for a high-ranking French ecclesiastic.

By 1456 or soon afterwards it had come into the collection of Piero, son of Cosimo de' Medici.

PSALTER

Venice, Biblioteca Marciana

LAT. I. 77 (= 2397), FOL. 21V

THIS MANUSCRIPT, as its title indicates, contains the Psalms, which are preceded by a calendar and followed by the canticles and litanies with prayers and the Office of the Dead. The first twenty-six leaves of the manuscript include twenty-four full-page miniatures. Eight of these illustrate episodes from the lives of various saints, and the remaining sixteen, inserted between the calendar and the Psalms, illustrate episodes from the lives of Mary and Jesus. The miniature shown here represents the Flight into Egypt. In addition to the miniatures, there are numerous historiated initials with biblical scenes concerning David and Solomon, as well as other simpler initials decorated with geometric motifs. The illuminator used copious amounts of gold and favoured red-purple and blue tones.

The script and the style of decoration suggest that the manuscript, a de luxe copy which presupposes a high-level patron, was made in the seventh to eighth decade of the thirteenth century in southern England, and more precisely in the diocese of Chichester. Furthermore, the fact that the saints include Sir Richard Wych, the Bishop of Chichester, canonized in 1262, but that the feast of his translation, which took place in 1276, is absent, provides chronological limits for the production of the manuscript. The representation of devout women in some of the initials of the Psalms has led to the hypothesis that the manuscript was created for use by women.

The codex came to Italy in the fifteenth century, but nothing further is known of its history until it was acquired by the Venetian bookseller and merchant Amedeo Svajer, whose heirs sold it, in 1794, to the Biblioteca Marciana.

ALFONSO THE WISE, Cantigas de Santa Maria

Florence, Biblioteca Nazionale Centrale

BANCO RARI 20, FOLS. 1, 18

ALFONSO X, KING OF CASTILE (1221–1284), the son of Ferdinand III and Beatrix of Swabia, was one of the most enlightened sovereigns of his time. He set greater store by cultural interests than by politics: he was a patron of musicians and poets, appreciated literature and science and wrote legal and historical works, as well as scientific works and poetry. His Song Book, which fuses together motifs drawn from Latin and vernacular collections of poetry, contains more than four hundred compositions.

In the manuscript which contains the *Cantigas*, written in Galician dialect and in metric forms of enormous variety, each composition is accompanied by one or even two illuminated pages. These are divided into six sections and framed by borders of geometric motifs interrupted by coats of arms. Ninety-one out of the total of 131 leaves are illuminated, but not all of them were completed: some lack the decorative border, in others colour has not been applied, others again have been left unfinished with the drawings of the figures and frames barely sketched.

On the left of the miniature on fol. 1, the Virgin and Child and two angels are opening the gates to Heaven and on the right King Alfonso is showing the scene to a crowd. Fol. 18, formed of six panels, represents a marine landscape. The first four scenes portray a ship in stormy waters, the fifth shows its arrival in port, and in the last is seen the thanksgiving of the travellers to the Virgin. The illustrations are on a small scale, but show a very careful attention to detail in the rendering of human figures, objects and architecture, suggesting the hand of a fine artist with an eye for detail. The scenes with figures are accompanied by initials with foliate motifs entwined with monstrous animals.

The style of the miniatures, executed by various artists who show French influence, suggests that the manuscript was made in Spain at the end of the thirteenth century and possibly intended for a high-ranking figure at the royal court.

ROLANDO DA PARMA, Chirurgia

Rome, Biblioteca Casanatense

1382, FOLS. 19, 23V, 2

THE MANUSCRIPT, WHICH IS DATABLE to the end of the thirteenth century, contains the complete text of the *Chirurgia* (Surgery) of Rolando da Parma, laid out in two columns. It is followed by other medical texts.

Rolando da Parma, a member of the Capezzuti family, lived in Bologna in the first half of the thirteenth century. In his work he reformulated the surgical writings of Ruggero da Furgardo, who had codified the fundamental norms of the teaching of surgery in the second half of the twelfth century. Rolando's reworking differs from its source in that he corrects and amplifies some parts of it, and adds symptomatology and diagnosis to surgery.

The resulting work became the basis of surgical teaching at the Medical School of Salerno, the oldest medieval institution in the European West for the teaching and practice of medicine. Salerno, a wealthy port at the crossing point of Mediterranean trade routes, became the cradle of Western medicine.

The miniatures in this manuscript form one of the oldest known examples of scientific illustration; they are not lavish, but they are perfectly preserved.

The work can be attributed to southern Italy on the grounds of the pictorial technique and the very bright colours used. The three miniatures shown here represent respectively the treatment of a dislocated neck; the treatment of discharged bowels by applying a disembowelled dog to the wound; then a series of figures with Hippocrates examining urine presented by an assistant in the presence of the patient; Hippocrates again, teaching a pupil to forge cauteries; and others illustrating the application of various cauteries.

ASTROLOGICAL TREATISE

Vatican City, Biblioteca Apostolica Vaticana

REG. LAT. 1283, FOL. 2V

THIS ASTROLOGICAL TREATISE in Spanish is based in part on the *Ghaiat*, an extensive compilation of uncertain date and authorship, which is traditionally attributed to Maslama ibn Ahmad al-Magritti, the most important mathematician and astronomer of Arab Spain in the eleventh century.

In 1256 the *Ghaiat* was translated from Arabic into Spanish on the order of Alfonso X, King of Castile.

The decoration of the Vatican manuscript consists of the signs of the zodiac accompanied by the constellations situated to their north and south. On fol. 2v, shown here, the sign of Gemini is represented in the centre surrounded by the constellations related to this zodiacal sign set in the outer segments.

The manuscript is datable to the late thirteenth or early fourteenth century.

tize duelo. El qui nasciere enel sera omne religioso ꞇ de muchas oraciones ꞇ fazara en fazer plazer a dios.

E nel ·xxvii· grado sube una uaca que yaze echada. El qui nasciere en el sera alfagem o estertolero.

E nel ·xxix· grado sube un omne que sopla fuego. El qui nasciere en el sera alcahuet ꞇ de muy mala noluntar.

E nel ·xxx· grado sube un omne que tiene en la mano un can toro. El qui nasciere en el sera mentiroso ꞇ muy malo ꞇ in fortunado.

femenino.

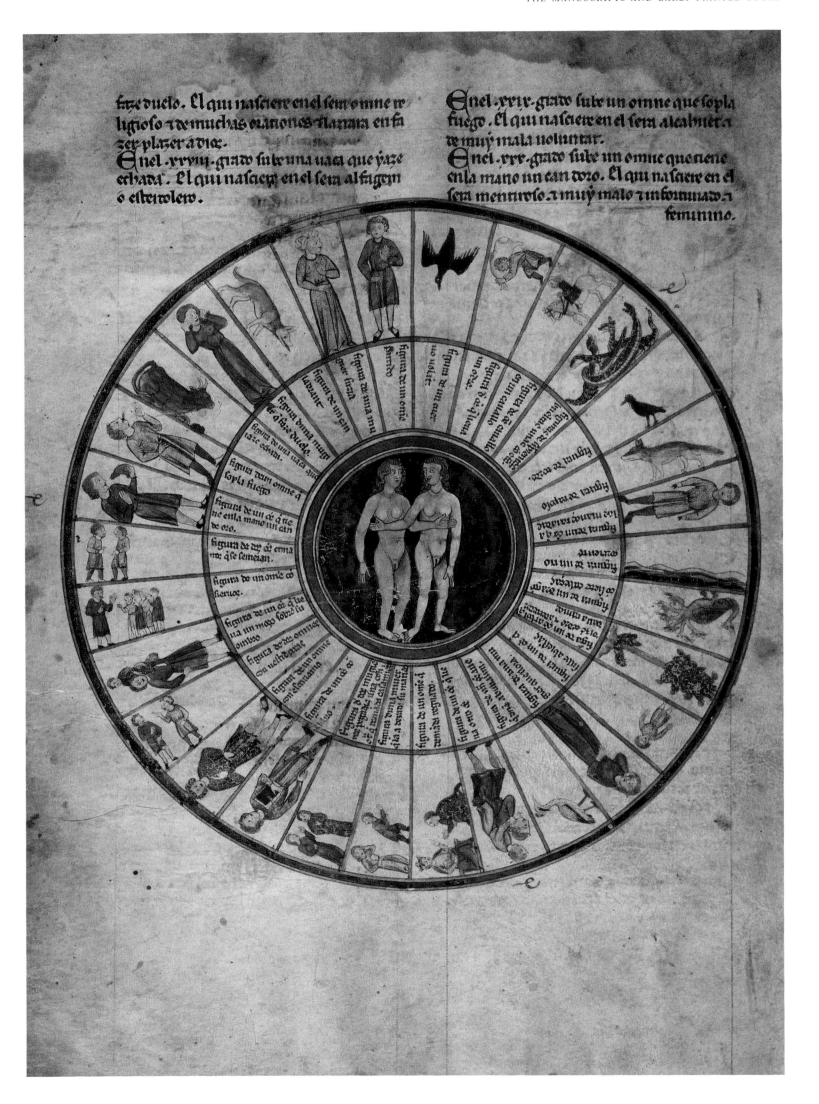

FRÈRE LAURENT, Somme le Roy

Modena, Biblioteca Estense

EST. 34 (= α. P. 8. 6), FOLS. 46, 59V, 97V

THE MAIN TEXT CONTAINED in this French manuscript, which is imperfect at the beginning and lacks leaves at the beginning of several chapters, is a medieval moral treatise, also known as *Somme des vices et des vertus* or *Cathechismus Gallicus*. A note on fol. 104v tells us that the text was composed in 1279, at the request of King Philip III of France, by a member of the friars preachers, who has been identified as the Dominican Frère Laurent, the King's confessor. The work circulated widely and was translated into Provençal, Italian, Spanish, Catalan, and English. The treatise is followed, from fols. 105 to 115, by another short moral work dealing with the remedies for vices and virtues by a different author, probably an imitator of Frère Laurent.

The manuscript, written in two columns, is illustrated by seven allegorical-didactic miniatures in rectangular frames, set in the width of either one or two columns of text. Fol. 46 shows the descent of the Holy Spirit. Fol. 59v represents Hope with the *Agnus Dei* above, and below Moses, who is separating two contendants, beside Noah's Ark. Fol. 97v has three scenes representing sobriety and gluttony. On the left, a temperate man is giving alms to a leper; on the right, the upper scene shows a rich man at a table cutting bread beside two figures in conversation; in the scene below, sobriety is represented by a woman on a lion holding a bird, with the glutton and a further figure sitting at a table in front of her.

The manuscript, which was produced in France in the fourteenth century, is not very refined either in its drawing or in its somewhat dull colouring.

lymage de la gloire ou il verra dieu
si come il est la qle uue serui
corone sanz fin ⁊ tout le loier des
sains ce serui tor le bien come dit
hue de s. victor uoir home qui
tout home fist ⁊ forma. Car por
co uolt diex deuenir home qͥl feist
⁊fourma. Car puis uolt diex de
uenir home qͥl feist en soi uenir
re tout home encors ⁊ en ame por
ce q home le ueust des rey du ciel
en su mauite · ⁊ lame lauerst en
sa dette si qͥl trouuast delui ⁊ dou
cour en son creatour por dedenz
⁊ par dehors en humanite ce serui
la gloire come ce serui sa ioie son
delit ⁊ uie pdurable q cele beneu
re uision ce serui la beneurte qͥ al
aiender q ᵗ uet dedenz ⁊ de cors.

Ci doiuent estre les ymages de so
brire ⁊ de glotonie ⁊ le riche au
disner ⁊ le ladre alaporte. Et le
riche qui demande la goute d eau
ue. Ci doit une dame en ce
lens sus .I. lyon q tient .I.
oissel ⁊ an ᵈ Sobriete. Et deuant
la dame doit auoir .I. home seat
a une table qui an ᵈ gloutonie
⁊ griete por la guelle. Et des
soz la dame doit auoir .I. home
seant a table q tenille son con pai
por mesure. Et de soz glotonie
doit auoir .I. home Et une fa
me seant a table. ⁊ la fame
fer sembler de coiner au mostre
au ladre. Et li home deffent
qͥ ne ait por ⁊ li hue les chi
es ⁊ li chien le chacent hors.

DANTE ALIGHIERI, Divine Comedy

Venice, Biblioteca Marciana

IT. IX. 276 (= 6902), FOLS. 58V, 53V

THIS FAMOUS FOURTEENTH-CENTURY CODEX is very large in format (430 x 280 mm) and extensively decorated with large initials at the beginning of each canto and with 170 miniatures, some of them full-page, distributed among the text, which is laid out in two columns.

The manuscript was formerly attributed simply to the Paduan and Venetian region, but it has since been recognized as Venetian from the style of the decoration, with its complex arabesques and the use of pale pink, yellow and blue in the skies of Hell. Chromatism is, indeed, of primary importance in the first part of the manuscript: it is so independent of the subjects represented that the tones used in the garments of Virgil and Dante vary even within a single scene, when the figures appear more than once.

The hand of a second artist can be seen in some pages in which the style is more plastic but less refined, and there is also a third hand, characterized by simpler and more arid drawing.

The illuminators of this manuscript signed it with their initials; one of them has been identified as Jacopo da Verona. The two miniatures shown here illustrate Cantos VI and I of Paradise: the first (fol. 58v) shows Beatrice and Dante, who is in conversation with Charles Martel; in the second (fol. 53v) Beatrice is pointing out the sun to Dante.

In the seventeenth century the manuscript was in the library of Francesco Loredan, who gave it to the Benedictine monks of the monastery on the island of San Giorgio Maggiore in Venice. It was carried off by the French at the end of the eighteenth century following the Napoleonic invasion and restored to Italy in 1816, when it was assigned to the Biblioteca Marciana.

RASIS, Liber medicinalis Almansoris,
translated into Italian by Zucchero Bencivenni

Florence, Biblioteca Medicea Laurenziana

PLUT. 73. 43, FOL. 6V

THE LITTLE THAT WE KNOW of Zucchero Bencivenni, a Florentine notary, derives from notes in his works which show that he was active between 1300 and 1313.

His main interest was in medical and astronomical texts. In 1300 he translated *Liber medicinalis Almansoris*, the famous medical text by the renowned ninth-century Islamic doctor Rasis, into Italian; the work had already been translated into Latin by Gerard of Cremona.

This manuscript of his translation is datable to the early fourteenth century. It is written in two columns and contains four miniatures on fol. 6v, following the index. In the first Rasis is shown presenting his work to King Almansor; in the second he is examining urine; in the last two he is examining and treating patients.

LIVRE DES SAINTS

Modena, Biblioteca Estense

EST. 116 (= α. T. 4. 14), FOLS. 126, 128

THE COMPLETE TITLE OF THE WORK, written on the first leaf of the manuscript, is *Livre des saints apostres, des saints martirs et confessors et des saintes vierges et de la nativite de notre dame sainte marie*. The text includes the story of the birth of Mary, accounts of several miracles of the Virgin, passages on the childhood of Jesus, accounts of the Assumption of Mary, and of the lives and miracles of numerous saints.

The text is laid out in two columns and has fifty-four miniatures filling the width of one column, the same number of initials decorated with geometric and foliate motifs, and one inhabited initial.

In some miniatures it is possible to make out preparatory notes written in the Venetian dialect which have not been painted over with colour and suggest that the manuscript was made in Venice. The figurative cycle, datable to the first decades of the fourteenth century, is particularly complex, because miniatures with pale, typically Byzantine colours are found alongside Romanesque style decoration using brighter colours. A third illuminator, whose work predominates in the manuscript alongside that of other more or less original hands, favoured elongated figures set against a background of dense, dark colours in the red, purple and bright green range. At the end of the manuscript the forms are more refined and distinct and take on typically fourteenth-century characteristics. The three saints represented in the small panel on fol. 126 are Protus, Hyacinth and Eugenia. The detail of fol. 128 shows Saint Sylvester, wearing bishop's robes, blessing the Emperor Constantine.

The codex belonged to Tommaso Obizzi del Catajo, whose coat of arms is found on the inside of the front board of the binding; it passed from him to the Este family by inheritance at the beginning of the nineteenth century.

DECRETUM GRATIANI

Vatican City, Biblioteca Apostolica Vaticana

VAT. LAT. 1366, FOL. 198

THIS IS A TYPICAL BOLOGNESE MANUSCRIPT, both in its script, the work of one hand, and in its decoration. It contains the *Decretum Gratiani*, a work of canon law composed towards 1140 to 1142. The *Glossa ordinaria* by Bartholomew of Brescia, who lived between the end of the twelfth and the first half of the thirteenth century, has been added in the margins. The work of Bartholomew, which occupies an important place in the history of canon law, is a revision of the *Apparatus* to the *Decretum* of Johannes Teutonicus, written shortly after the Lateran Council of 1215. Bartholomew's *Glossa ordinaria* eventually superseded the work from which it was derived, so much so that the *Apparatus* survives in only a few manuscripts and is not included in any printed edition.

The illumination of the Vatican codex has recently been attributed to a group of Bolognese artists from the fourteenth-century, among whom predominates the 'Master of 1328', who decorated the first leaf, and the 'Illustrator' and his workshop, to whom the miniature shown here is attributed. It depicts a young girl taking the veil. The choice of bright colours and the unusual positioning of the figures, who emerge from the margins to give the scene plastic movement, are typical of this artist.

The large number of artists who worked on the manuscript combined with the lack of decoration on many pages have led scholars to believe that the patron must have taken the manuscript away when he left Bologna.

MISSAL

Venice, Biblioteca Marciana

LAT. III. III, FOLS. 60V, 131

THE CODEX, imperfect at the beginning and end, and damaged by damp in some parts, was produced for the Basilica of San Marco in Venice. The decoration, found on almost every page, consists of border frames made up of foliate motifs, miniatures with scenes from the Bible and the lives of the saints, and a large, full-page Crucifixion.

The presence of Paduan and Emilian stylistic features, the evidence of Byzantine and Venetian influence, and the varied ways in which the figures are drawn, have led critics to conclude that the decoration was the work of a number of artists from different schools. Recently scholars have suggested that the manuscript was produced in Venice in the 1320s.

The original binding of the codex is now kept separately: the wooden boards are covered with silver gilt, engraved with the figures of Christ, the Virgin and several saints. It is thought that the binding was executed in the thirteenth century and later adapted for this Missal.

PSALTER

Naples, Biblioteca Vittorio Emanuele III

I. B. 50, FOL. 14

THE MANUSCRIPT, which consists of 150 leaves containing the text of the Psalms, is small in format (170 x 120 mm) but of excellent artistic quality. Its decoration consists of eight illuminated initials inhabited by small figures (mainly biblical, but also symbolical and clerical), in which the elegance of the drawing is underlined by the choice of chromatic tones that stand out against arabesque or chequered grounds in lighter colours. Delicate borders framing the pages are enriched with buds and small leaves, or with fantastic animals and little birds.

On fol. 14, in the initial 'B' at the beginning of the Psalm *Beatus vir*, David is shown playing the lyre. At the bottom, along the sober and elegant frame, the small figure of a huntsman sounding his horn and a deer hunted by two dogs are highlighted by the careful use of shadow.

The decoration as a whole, the delicate, confident drawing, the harmonious colours, the elegance of the borders, as well as the refined, red and blue ornamental design of the lesser initials, which are enlivened by touches of gold, suggests that the hand behind the fine illumination must have been one the most able followers of Jean Pucelle. Pucelle, the main representative of the Paris school in the first half of the fourteenth century, produced wonderful works for the French court.

BOETHIUS,
De arithmetica, De musica
Naples, Biblioteca Vittorio Emanuele III

V. A. 14, FOLS. 46V-47

BOTH THE PAGES SHOWN HERE from this beautiful manuscript, which dates from the mid-fourteenth century, are decorated with full-page scenes.

The left-hand page shows the Lord enthroned holding the keys in his left hand. The figure is enclosed in a mandorla, which is supported by four angels and surrounded by seven candlesticks. The symbols of the four Evangelists are depicted in the corners of the page.

The facing page is devoted to the representation of music. In the centre a female figure personifying the art is shown surrounded by smaller figures playing various musical instruments; they are dominated by King David, set in a circle at the top.

The manuscript was copied by a Franciscan monk from Naples during the period of the Angevin domination.

The decoration, which is very carefully executed, was formerly attributed either to a Sienese illuminator active in Naples or to an artist belonging to Matteo Giovannetti's school at Avignon. More recently, however, a strong French element has been noted in the execution of the figures, especially those illustrating music. A comparison has been made with some paintings in the Palais des Papes at Avignon and it has been suggested that the manuscript was produced in this cultural environment.

BENOÎT DE SAINTE MAURE,
Roman de Troie

Venice, Biblioteca Marciana

FR. Z. 17 (= 230), FOL. 21V

B ENOÎT DE SAINTE MAURE, a French twelfth-century poet, was probably a vassal of King Henry II, for whom he wrote the 43,000-verse
Chronique des ducs de Normandie. His most famous work, however, is the
Roman de Troie, written between 1160 and 1165. It draws on the Latin works
of Dares Phrygius and Dictys Cretensis, but its style is very personal and
the amorous episodes are treated with great imagination.

The manuscript was produced in northern Italy between about 1330
and 1340. The text is laid out in two columns and there are miniatures on
almost every page.

The scenes shown here, on fol. 21v, show the embassy of Antenor to
Greece.

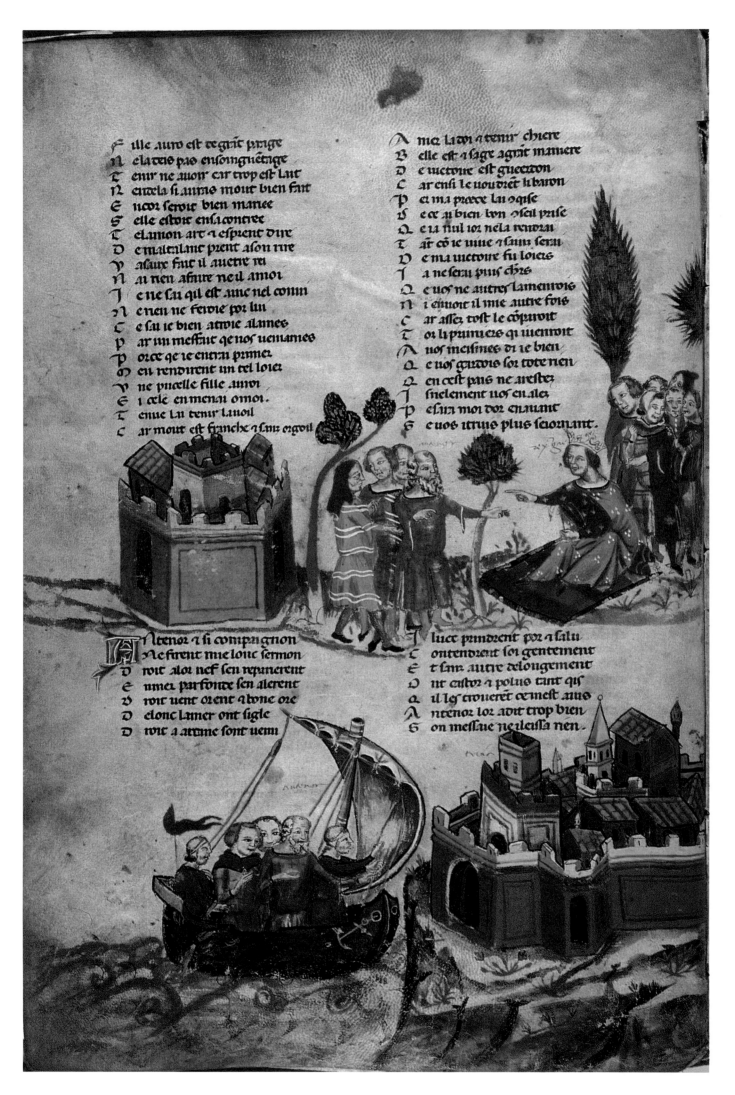

HUNGARIAN ANGEVIN LEGENDARY

Vatican City, Biblioteca Apostolica Vaticana

VAT. LAT. 8541, FOL. 80

THIS CODEX, datable to about 1333, now consists of only part of what there must have been in the original manuscript. The Vatican manuscript has 106 leaves; further leaves, containing eighty-five miniatures, are now in the Pierpont Morgan Library in New York, five leaves are kept in the Collection of Drawings at the Hermitage in St Petersburg, and it is probable that further miniatures are lost.

The decoration of each page consists of four scenes, framed and accompanied by captions giving an account of the lives of the saints. Although each is autonomous, they are nevertheless linked by their content.

The illumination shows clear Bolognese influence and appears to have been executed by three or four artists: they were probably either Italian masters working in Hungary or Hungarian illuminators who had trained in Bologna.

Analysis of the text shows that the Legendary was designed for use in Hungary; numerous saints who are important in the Hungarian liturgy are included and the manuscript can be linked more specifically to the cultural circle of the Angevin court of Buda. It is possible that it was commissioned for the education of Prince Andrew (the second son of Carobert of Anjou, who was taken by his father to Naples in the hope that he would succeed to the Angevin throne), and that the project was entrusted to a learned cleric.

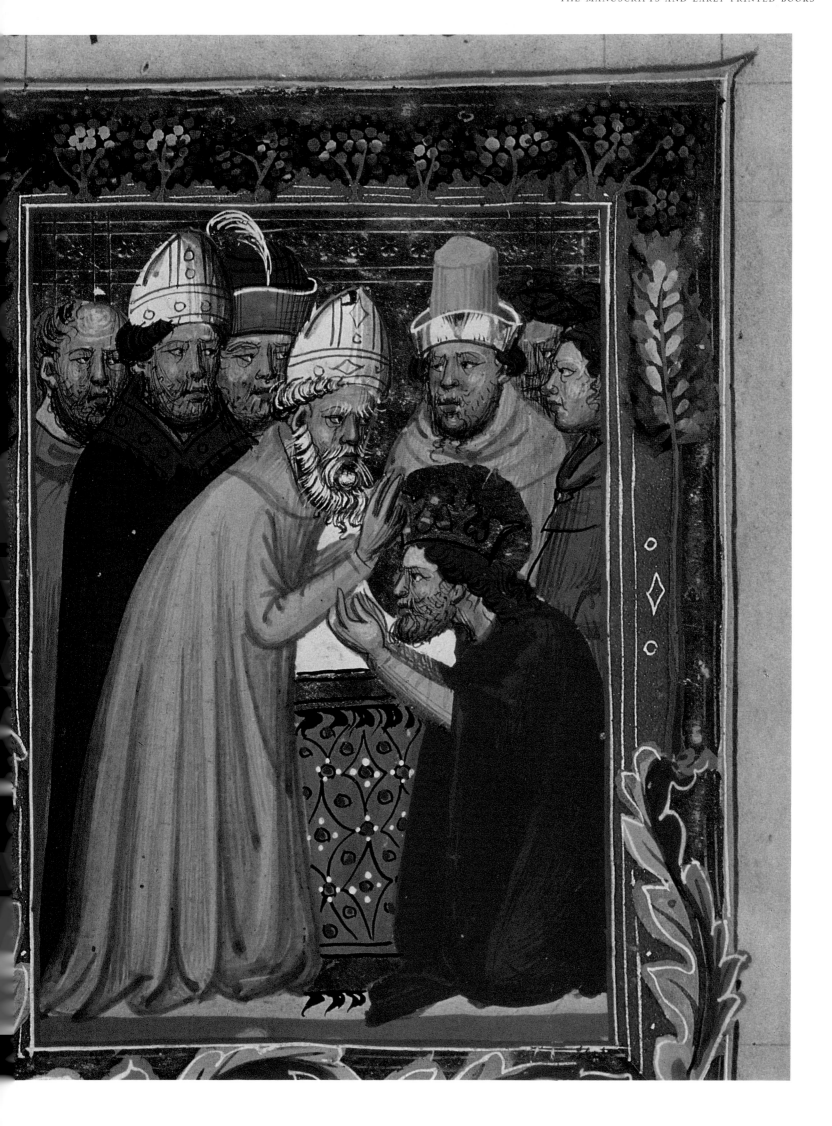

CONVENEVOLE DA PRATO,
Panegyric in honour of King Robert of Anjou

Florence, Biblioteca Nazionale Centrale

BANCO RARI 38, FOLS. 4V-5, 10V

THE MANUSCRIPT CONTAINS an anonymous verse poem written at the beginning of the fourteenth century (circa 1320) eulogizing King Robert of Anjou (1278–1343). The author, who describes himself as a teacher and poet from Prato, has been identified as Petrarch's master, Convenevole da Prato (1270/1275–1338).

Of the thirty-six leaves in the codex, thirty contain miniatures, some including single figures and others showing groups. On fol. 4v, Christ in Majesty holds the terrestrial globe showing the three continents (Europe, Asia, Africa) in his left hand; the facing page (fol. 5) presents the Virgin in prayer at the top of a short flight of steps, at the bottom of which is a dragon representing the devil. The miniature on fol. 10v, representing Robert of Anjou sitting on a throne and holding the globe, has a monumental character reminiscent of panel and fresco painting. The plasticity of the painting of his face, which is depicted with care, is highlighted by a masterful use of chiaroscuro. The blue ground is enriched with gold-leaf fleur-de-lis, a symbol found in the arms of the House of Anjou. Scholars have suggested that this manuscript was given to Robert of Anjou by the magistrates of Prato; it has been dated between 1334 and 1336.

Although the decoration is considered to have been executed by artists of a Florentine workshop whose style is close to that of Taddeo Gaddi, one of Giotto's pupils, not all the work is of the same quality. Three different hands are discernible.

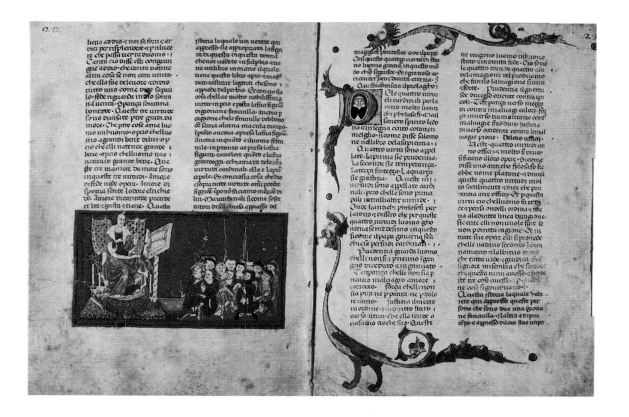

ZUCCHERO BENCIVENNI,
Translation of the Somme le Roy into Italian

Florence, Biblioteca Nazionale Centrale

II. VI. 16, FOLS. II V-12, 73

ZUCCHERO BENCIVENNI, who was active at the beginning of the fourteenth century, made translations into both Italian and Latin. Although he was interested in medicine and astrology (see p. 72), the principal work for which he is famous, his translation of the *Somme le Roy*, is not scientific. This wide-ranging French text, in which the teachings of moral philosophy are enriched by pungent references to contemporary society, was composed in 1279, as can be seen from a note in the manuscript itself (see also p. 68).

The manuscript, copied in two columns, is decorated with numerous images illustrating and explaining the text. Some critics consider that the work was executed by three illuminators active in or near Florence in the 1370s, while others believe it was executed by Pisan artists in the 1340s.

The second hypothesis is supported by the typology of the complex border decoration (consisting of acanthus leaves interspersed with the heads of fantastic animals, with dragons with human faces and with grotesque faces (fol. 12). The first illuminator, who decorated fols. 1–40v, depicts strongly realistic and animated scenes, with a highly expressionistic force in the representation of human features. The second illuminator decorated the part of the text dealing with the works of mercy; the scenes are inspired by popular tradition and have marked outlines and strong colours. Fol. 73 was executed by the third illuminator: the scene portrays an allegory of Temperance, personified by a woman wearing a pink garment who is standing on a lion and holding six doves, symbolizing the six Virtues.

145

et nellanima iluedesse ifua
deita sichelli tiouasse dol
core et diseto asuo eiatoe
dentio nela deita disuoii
dentio nela deita disuoii
nellumanita Cio saiie
lagloria duomo Cio saiie
sua suo disocto tutto suo
diseto quita pontabile che
quella beata iisione labea
titudine che quelli attedono
che guardano nectecta di
core dicorpo Questa isto
na perdimostiare una no
bile figura laquale efiguia
ta asimilitudine disobrieta
laquale edimolta uirtude
plasia nobilitade siposano
in lei queste bi uirtudi di
che abbiamo parlato ique
sto libro Et sicome loleone

sopia stie pnatura per po
tentia uniuersalmente atut
te fieie saluatiche opimesti
che Cosi sobrietate etaneta
uirtude che tutte queste bi
uirtudi siposano inlei ti
questi colombi iquali sipo
no insu lebraccia dique fi
gura sono assimighati ale
bi uirtudi ti po che queste
uirtudi ploro natura pote
tia mantengono lanima
pura aneta nelcospecto di
dio po figuiamo questi nc
celli acolombi bianchi aecio
che cosa biancha ae proprieta
de dipurita di inectecta
i pcio che queste nobilissie
uirtudi sobrieta leneeue
inse medesemo conanimo
affectuo po tutte bi siposcoilei

73

BENOÎT DE SAINTE MAURE, Roman de Troie

Vatican City, Biblioteca Apostolica Vaticana

REG. LAT. 1505, FOL. 197V

T HE MANUSCRIPT CONTAINS the French translation, completed in about 1160 by Benoît de Sainte Maure, of the *De bello troiano* by Dictys Cretensis and the *Excidio Troiae* by Dares Phrygius.

The first sixteen leaves of the codex were copied at the end of the thirteenth century, while the remainder was added at the beginning of the fourteenth century. Linguistic analysis suggests that the work was transcribed in Italy by two scribes who knew little French, copying a manuscript with good textual readings.

Almost all the leaves are illustrated with miniatures executed by a number of artists who were not particularly expert. It may be that they were painters rather than illuminators, since the scenes extend beyond the spaces designated for them. Fol. 197v shows the Greeks offering the wooden horse to the Trojans.

The style of clothing worn by the figures suggests that the decoration was completed between 1340 and 1350, perhaps in north-central Italy since it includes several Bolognese or Genoese elements.

Before the manuscript passed into the possession of Queen Christina of Sweden, it belonged to Pierre Michon Bourdelot, who was her doctor between 1651 and 1653 and sold his library to the Queen.

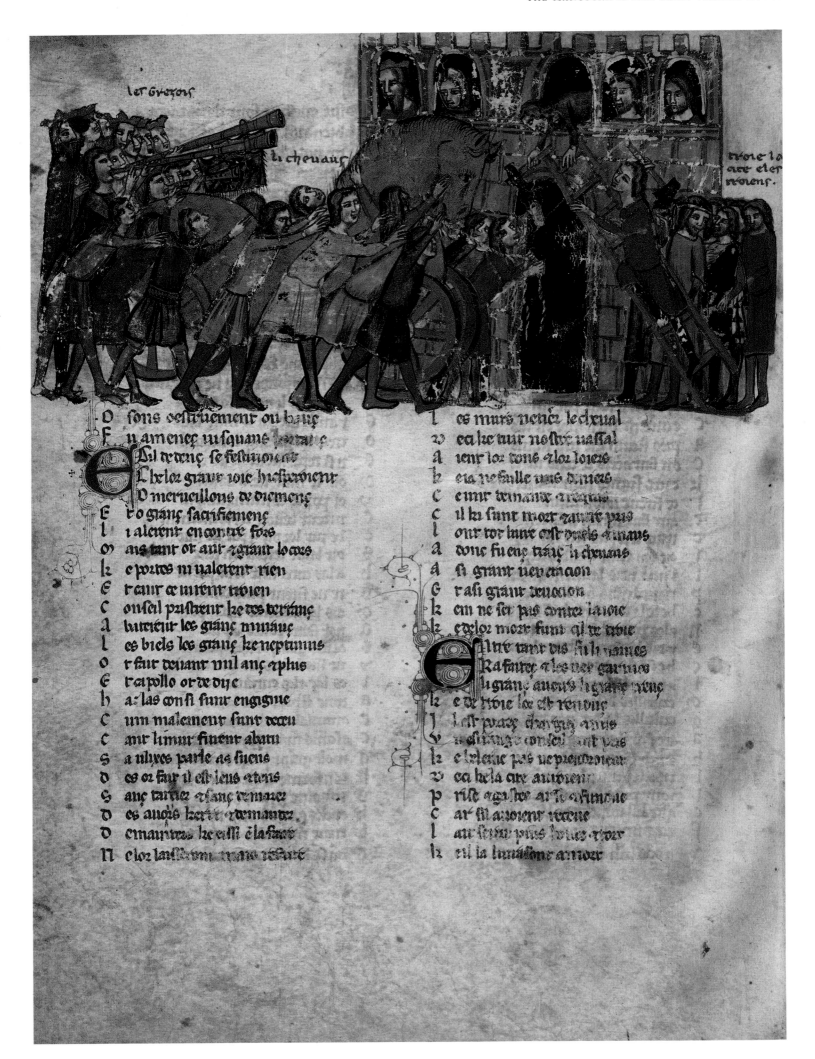

GREGORY IX, Decretals

Ravenna, Biblioteca Classense

488, FOLS. 143V, 4

THE MANUSCRIPT IS COMPOSITE: the first two leaves are later than the rest and are datable between 1370 and 1380. The original manuscript was made between about 1340 and 1350.

The first two leaves contain tables of consanguinity and comments on the Fourth Book of the *Decretals* of Gregory IX by Giovanni d'Andrea, who was a canonist and law teacher at Bologna and Padua at the beginning of the fourteenth century. Fol. 4 is decorated with a miniature showing the table of consanguinity. At the centre of a green, three-dimensional grid, a large ancestral figure is depicted with a tree-shaped schema before him, which outlines the grades of relationship in which marriage was forbidden without ecclesiastical dispensation. This graphic representation derives from the geometric diagrams found in medieval codices which illustrated the blood relationships established for inheritance by Roman law. The miniature has been attributed to Matteo di Ser Cambio, an artist who worked in Perugia in whom Sienese and Paduan influences are merged.

The rest of the manuscript, which contains the text of the *Decretals*, is ornamented with decorated initials and scenes with figures. Fol. 143v shows the Adoration of the Host. The style of illumination in this part of the manuscript localizes it securely in Perugia in the second quarter of the fourteenth century; the decoration is particularly close to a manuscript produced in the *scriptorium* of San Lorenzo.

DOMENICO LENZI,
Specchio umano (Biadaiolo)

Florence, Biblioteca Medicea Laurenziana

TEMPI 3, FOLS. 7, 58

IN THIS MANUSCRIPT the author, the corn merchant Domenico Lenzi, listed the prices of grain and fodder sold at Orsanmichele in Florence. There are also accounts of the working of the market, the political economy of the Comune, the riots in various Tuscan towns following the famine of 1328–1330, and other important events in Florence such as the flood of 1333. The historical narrative is interspersed with thirty-eight sections in verse, some of which are linked to the subject of the work, while others explain the illustrations and still others appear to be mere space fillers. This work, which is both composite and unique of its kind, cannot be classified in any of the literary categories of the late Middle Ages. The subject of the work is Florence, and particularly the market at Orsanmichele, and a moralistic lesson for the reader underlies the subject matter.

We know nothing of Domenico Lenzi and it is unclear who commissioned the work. One hypothesis is that it was the author himself; other scholars believe the work was produced for the Arte della Lana (Wool Guild), to which Lenzi belonged.

The decoration, consisting of nine miniatures by an anonymous painter known as the 'Maestro del Biadaiolo', is of great interest. There are pictures of grain dealing, a merchant at his accounts in front of buyers, threshing, reaping and the Orsanmichele market in times of plenty (fol. 7) and famine. The representation of the expulsion of the poor from Siena and their entrance into Florence (fol. 58) is of particular interest. This miniature shows numerous Florentine buildings: the city walls, the gate of the Bishop's Palace, the church of Santa Reparata, the campanile of the church of the Badia, the Giotto campanile under construction, the Baptistery and the tower of the Bargello. From the architectural features shown in this miniature it is possible to date the manuscript to the years between 1344 and 1347.

BARTOLOMEO DA SAN CONCORDIO,
Teachings of the ancients

Florence, Biblioteca Nazionale Centrale

II. II. 319, FOL. 3; PAL. 600, FOL. 63; II. II.319, FOL. 36

BARTOLOMEO DA SAN CONCORDIO, a Dominican friar who lived between 1262 and 1347, composed a treatise *De documentis antiquarum*, of which he himself made an Italian version with the title *Ammaestramenti degli antichi* (Teachings of the ancients). It contains approximately 2,000 religious and civil precepts.

The two codices in the Biblioteca Nazionale in Florence both contain the vernacular version of the work. Analysis of the decoration suggests that both manuscripts were illuminated in the workshop of Jacopo da Casentino, a painter and illuminator who died in 1349.

Of the miniatures shown here two, the initial 'S' on fol. 3 in which four figures are represented (the first is a portrait of the author wearing the Dominican habit) and the Wheel of Fortune on fol. 36, are taken from the first codex MS. II.II.319, dated 1342. On fol. 63 of MS. Pal. 600, the initial 'D' contains the figure of a young man pointing with a dagger to the text concerning sin.

BOOK OF HOURS (Visconti Hours)

Florence, Biblioteca Nazionale Centrale

BANCO RARI 397, FOL. 117V

THE MANUSCRIPT, known as the Visconti Hours or Offiziolo visconteo, is one of the most famous illuminated codices in the Biblioteca Nazionale. It contains the first part of this book of Hours: the second part is to be found in MS. Landau Finaly 22 in the same library (see p. 124). It is not thought that one original codex was dismembered: the large number of leaves makes it likely that the text was divided into two parts which were bound separately from the beginning.

The manuscript was made for Gian Galeazzo Visconti (1351–1402), the ruler of Milan from 1385. His coat of arms, consisting of a large snake which intersects the capital letters and mingles with the decorative motifs and border decoration, can be seen on many pages, accompanied by his portrait in profile in the lower margins.

The manuscript was written by a certain brother Amadeus, and splendidly decorated by the Lombard illuminator Giovannino de' Grassi, whose style is clearly discernible in the architectural features often used to form the initials, in the landscapes in the lower margins of the pages, in the careful representation of animals, and in the human figures in which pink and blue tones predominate.

By 1389 when Giovannino began working for Milan Cathedral the Offiziolo must already have been completed. Some scholars believe that work on it began in 1370 (the date appears on fol. 2, in the scene showing the expulsion of Joachim and Anna from the temple), while others would postpone the start on the decoration to 1378 or 1379, on the basis of allusions to episodes from the life of Gian Galeazzo contained in the miniatures.

The miniature shown here is of David enthroned.

HISTOIRES

Venice, Biblioteca Marciana

FR. Z. 2 (= 223), FOLS. 9, 190V

THE CODEX, written by a single scribe in a version of French mixed with Venetian terms, contains a compendium of history from the Creation to Roman times, as we are informed by the complete title: *Histoires depuis le commencement du Monde jusqu'à la guerre de Mitridate et aux victoires de Pompée.*

It is thought to have been produced between 1380 and 1391, since both Gonzaga and Visconti devices are found in the manuscript; the marriage of Francesco Gonzaga and Agnese Visconti took place in 1380 and was brought to an end in 1391, when Agnese was accused of infidelity and killed.

Two illuminators worked on the decoration of the manuscript. The first artist decorated fol. 9, which shows the Gonzaga and Visconti family devices. The decoration by the second artist, who executed most of the manuscript including fol. 190v, consists of compositions arranged in four small squares per page.

The language of the text is of particular interest. It is only to be found in this manuscript and in another belonging to the Gonzaga family, and was used so that the text could more easily be understood by the circle of people for whom it was intended.

conques fuſſent. auʒ fu li temples
ianus clos. por ce quil nauoieſ mer
nu le bataille. Et ceſte choſe neſtoit
mais auenue des le tens q̄ numa
pompilius fu rois qui regna apres ro
mulus ſi con uos aueʒ oi ꞇ entendu
arriere. En ce temple ianus eſtoient
toutes les armes de rome miſes et

CECCO D'ASCOLI, Acerba

Florence, Biblioteca Medicea Laurenziana

PLUT. 40. 52, FOLS. 24V, 30

THE ACERBA, A DIDACTIC-ALLEGORICAL POEM in Italian, written in seven-syllable couplets, is the most famous work by Francesco Stabili, better known as Cecco d'Ascoli. He was a doctor and astrologer who lived between the second half of the thirteenth century and the first decades of the four-teenth century.

The text, which deals with celestial phenomena and influences, natural history and philosophical matters, is contained in the first seventy-seven leaves of this famous manuscript. It was written by a single scribe and embellished not only with penflourished red and blue initials, but also with skilfully exe-cuted illustrations, which scholars at the end of the nineteenth century already believed to have been one of the figurative sources of Leonardo da Vinci's *Bes-tiario* (now MS. Hamilton 138 in the Deutsche Staatsbibliothek in Berlin), which was decorated by a fifteenth-century Lombard artist.

The codex has been ascribed to the region of the Veneto, both on the basis of linguistic analysis, and because of the decoration; the colours and the skilful use of gold, which smacks of late Byzantine tradition, suggest a Venetian artist who is also accomplished at large-scale painting. This hypothesis is supported by the ease with which the artist executed large-scale figures, such as the female figures on fols. 24v and 30.

The manuscript has been dated to before 1390 on the basis of an emblem on fol. 1vv, which can be linked to Bonifacio Lupi, who died in that year and who may have commissioned the codex. Similar coats of arms can be seen outside the portico of the chapel of San Giacomo in the Basilica del Santo in Padua and on the tomb of Bonifacio Lupi himself. It has been suggested that the manuscript was transferred to Florence already at the time of his death, possi-bly by way of his Tuscan wife Caterina Franceschi.

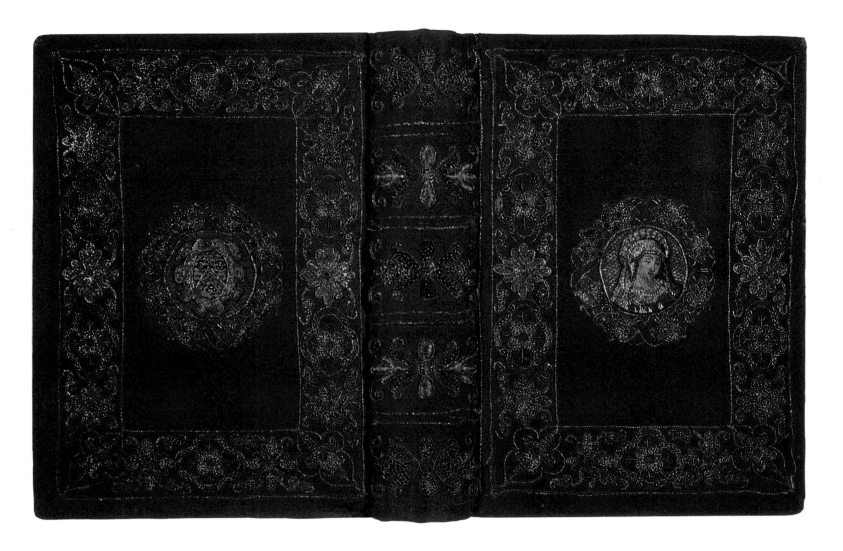

BOOK OF HOURS

Modena, Biblioteca Estense

LAT. 842 (= α. R. 7. 3), BINDING, FOL. 240

THE 272 LEAVES OF THIS SMALL CODEX, containing the offices for the Virgin, are decorated by borders with foliate motifs, historiated initials with scenes from the New Testament and twenty-eight full-page miniatures showing episodes from the lives of Christ, the Virgin, and the saints, including representations of Saint Sebastian, Saint Christopher crossing the river, Saint George killing the dragon, Saint Catherine, Saint Laurence and, on fol. 240, Saint Dorothy.

The author of the decoration is unknown, but was certainly a Lombard influenced by Giovannino de' Grassi and Anovelo da Imbonate.

The scribe, Anselmo Ronzio, also a Lombard, was a lawyer at the Papal Curia. He signed his name on fol. 267 of the manuscript, and noted that he finished his copy in 1390.

The binding of the manuscript, executed in the sixteenth century, is in red silk with embroidery in yellow, green and blue silk, and gold and silver thread. An image of the Virgin is embroidered in the centre of the front cover.

Before passing to the Biblioteca Estense in 1817, the manuscript belonged to Tommaso Obizzi del Catajo, whose *ex-libris* is written inside the cover.

TACUINUM SANITATIS

Rome, Biblioteca Casanatense

459, FOLS. 36, 33V

A TACUINUM IS A KIND OF ENCYCLOPAEDIA of natural sciences in which plants, animals and minerals are described in alphabetical order by sections, with particular reference to their healing properties.

Watercolour drawings in the upper part of each page illustrate the text which is laid out in two columns in the lower register. At the beginning of each section, the initial letter encloses a half-length human figure and a sumptuous border of flowers and leaves in bright colours and gold, often embellished with elegant architectural motifs, human figures or animals (such as that on fol. 36), frames the page. This type of decoration is complemented by numerous scenes, the most interesting of which portray farming and rural activities: a farmer who has picked pumpkins, the cleaning of barrels, sheep shearing, a milk seller and fishing. The entire decorative scheme, of the Lombard school of the end of the fourteenth century, is attributed to Giovannino de' Grassi and his assistants.

The manuscript was made for the Emperor Wenceslas of Luxembourg, who ascended the throne in 1378 and was deposed in 1400. His coat of arms with the imperial eagle was painted in the lower margin of the first page of the text, which is illustrated with a miniature representing the enthroned emperor with the six electors, surrounded by the cardinal and theological virtues.

The imperial coat of arms was overpainted with that of Matthias Corvinus when the manuscript entered the magnificent library of the King of Hungary, one of the richest and most outstanding collections of the second half of the fifteenth century, which was broken up on the death of the King. Numerous manuscripts once in the collection have been identified in libraries all over the world.

GRADUAL

Verona, Biblioteca Capitolare

MLXI, FOL. 40

THE MANUSCRIPT BELONGS to a double series of seventeen choir books, which were kept in the Cathedral of Verona until 1902, when they were transferred to the Biblioteca Capitolare. The original plan was for eighteen volumes: eight antiphonaries, containing the antiphons for the day and night offices, eight graduals, containing the sung part of the Mass with music, and two responsories (one is missing). A responsory is a book of liturgical chants in which the soloist and choir alternate.

The *corpus* of volumes was probably produced in two distinct phases: a first commission of eleven choir books is datable to the 1370s and 1380s; the remaining six, which are larger in size and decorated with greater care, were the result of a second commission towards the end of the century. The eighteenth volume, which was substituted for one either no longer in use or never executed, was copied at the beginning of the eighteenth century by Francesco Bellavite, a member of the family of famous Veronese goldsmiths.

The decoration of the earlier choir books, which constitutes one of the most important examples of fourteenth-century Veronese illumination, has been attributed to artists whose style can be compared with that of Turone di Maxio da Camnago, a painter of Lombard origin who is known especially for his polyptych in Castelvecchio, signed and dated 1360.

The page illustrated here belongs to one of the choir books of the second series: it is larger in size and the decoration is finer.

CHRONICA DE CARRARENSIBUS

Venice, Biblioteca Marciana

LAT. X. 381 (= 2802), FOLS. 1V-2

THE MANUSCRIPT CONTAINS two chronicles by an anonymous author, in Latin and Italian, concerning the Carrara family who ruled Padua, albeit with some interruptions, from 1318 to 1406.

Since this particularly opulent codex includes an invocation to Francesco Novello da Carrara, it is considered to have been dedicated to him. It was probably produced in the last decade of the fourteenth century and is decorated with four miniatures executed in Padua. Jacopo da Carrara is represented on fol. 1V as he draws his sword against Ezzellino da Romano in front of Frederick II in 1237. Fol. 2 shows a thronging crowd witnessing the election of Jacopo il Grande da Carrara as Captain of the People in 1318.

It is worth noting that Petrarch's second mission to Venice, in 1373, is mentioned in the vernacular chronicle.

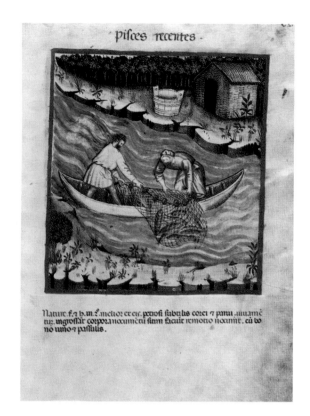

THEATRUM SANITATIS

Rome, Biblioteca Casanatense

4182, FOLS. 157, 100, 118

THE TEXT OF THIS MANUSCRIPT, which is datable to between the end of the fourteenth century and the beginning of the fifteenth century, is attributed to the Arabic doctor Ububchasym de Baldach. It can be classified as a *Tacuinum sanitatis*, that is a medical manual, deriving from erudite treatments, containing rules of hygiene, and sometimes descriptions of animals and plants which are useful to man. This literary genre underwent significant developments in the fourteenth and fifteenth centuries and it is a witness to the renewed interest in medicine that was sparked by Arabic culture.

In the Casanatense *Theatrum sanitatis*, after the title there is an explanation of the contents, outlining the six things necessary to every man for his health, with the various necessary rectifications and actions to be taken: air, food and drink, movement and rest, sleep and wakefulness, the humours, joy and anxiety. It is explained that all this information was collected into a book so that the reader could find useful information rather than erudite definitions, without having to rely on men of learning.

The text is illustrated by 208 miniatures arranged on both the recto and verso of each leaf. The scene on fol. 157 represents fishing; fol. 100 shows the shop of a drug seller and fol. 118 that of a salt seller. The miniatures, which help to make the text readily comprehensible, are attributed to the school of the Milanese artist Giovannino de' Grassi. They are particularly interesting for the architecture of the houses and shops, and for the landscapes that act as backgrounds to the scenes of daily life.

There are at least four other similar extant Tacuina: MS. Series Nova 2644 in the National Library in Vienna (which is the closest to the Casanatense manuscript in style and content), MS. Nouv. acq. lat. 1673 in the Bibliothèque Nationale in Paris, MS. 877 in Liège University Library, and MS. 3054 in the Municipal Library of Rouen.

The manuscript was bought for the Casanatense in 1773 from the bookseller Barrolowich.

CXVIII

· Sal ·

Natuie c. in j. s. in ʒ. melioz ex eo. adzuani. iuuamenti. facit abu de
sccdere 7 digeiere. nocumctiz. cerebzo 7 uisui. zemotio nocumenti.
lotus 7 tozrfactus.

BOOK OF HOURS FOR THE USE OF ROUEN

Naples, Biblioteca Nazionale Vittorio Emanuele III

I. B. 27, FOL. 85

THIS MANUSCRIPT, written in Latin and French, is a book of Hours for the use of Rouen, as can be seen from the calendar which precedes the text of the offices. The manuscript is illuminated with decorated initials accompanied by rich and ample borders of branches from which flowers and small leaves spring (sometimes interspersed with powerful figures of angels which decorate the borders of the text pages), and with forty large miniatures set in arched frames which depict saints and martyrs or stories taken from the gospels. The scene on fol. 85 shows the Annunciation to the Shepherds.

The miniatures provide little glimpses of daily life and are characterized by a strong naturalism, with picturesque landscapes and accurately drawn architecture, all painted in bright colours, among which blue, green and red predominate. These characteristics, typical of Franco-Flemish illumination, have been ascribed to Jacques Coene, the Flemish painter, illuminator and architect, who was active in the late fourteenth century and the first half of the fifteenth century both in Paris and in Milan, to which city he was expressly summoned in 1399 to work on the construction of the cathedral. Coene belonged to the circle of, and was perhaps a pupil of, the 'Master of the Hours of Marshal Boucicaut', or 'Boucicaut Master', whose influence is to be observed here not so much in the borders as in the miniatures, in whose execution Coene also made use of collaborators and in which he displays an ability to give an impression of space and depth in the landscapes.

The manuscript belonged to the Farnese library and was taken to Naples in 1736 by Carlo di Borbone.

DANTE ALIGHIERI,
Divine Comedy

Florence, Biblioteca Nazionale Centrale

BANCO RARI 215, FOLS. II, 78V

FROM NOTES ON FOL. 1 we learn that this fine fifteenth-century codex of the *Divine Comedy* was once owned by Francesco Sassetti (1421–1490), a Florentine merchant who was the administrator of the Geneva branch of the Medici Bank.

On fol. II a fine portrait of Dante sketched in pen differs from the rest of the decoration both stylistically and technically. The decoration of the codex also includes decorated initials and three full-page watercolour drawings.

On fol. IIIv Hell, Purgatory and Paradise are represented schematically. In the facing illustration (fol. IV), Dante is shown with the three wild beasts and meeting Virgil.

On fol. 78v, shown here, at the beginning of Purgatory, the third watercolour shows the Mount of Purgatory guarded by an angel and the meeting of Virgil and Dante with Cato.

CRISTOFORO BUONDELMONTI,
Liber insularum arcipelagi

Venice, Biblioteca Marciana

LAT. X. 123 (= 3784), FOL. 22

CRISTOFORO BUONDELMONTI was born in Florence in 1386 and spent most of his life, after he abandoned a career in the church, on journeys which took him to most of the islands of the Aegean.

He was an avid scholar of classical antiquity and collected a large number of codices. He wrote two geographical texts, *Descriptio insulae Cretae*, which he sent to the Florentine humanist Niccolò Niccoli in 1417, and *Liber insularum arcipelagi*, which he dedicated in 1420 to Cardinal Giordano Orsini.

The first version of his second work is lost, but he compiled later versions in 1420, 1422 and 1430. The *Liber* is arranged as a journey, with each chapter devoted to an island or place and provided with maps and historical, archaeological and mythological digressions.

This copy of the text dates from the fifteenth century and contains thirty-two maps. The one shown here represents Constantinople: one can see the city walls, the river Lycus, Hagia Sophia, the Hippodrome, the Imperial Palace of Blachernai and the columns of Constantine and Theodosius. The Genoese district of Pera is shown at the top.

BOOK OF HOURS (Visconti Hours)

Florence, Biblioteca Nazionale Centrale

LANDAU FINALY 22, FOL. 70

TOGETHER WITH MS BANCO RARI 397 (see p. 102), this manuscript makes up the famous Offiziolo Visconteo, the book of Hours commissioned by the Visconti family. Because of its exceptional decoration it is considered to be one of the masterpieces of Lombard miniature.

Like its companion volume, it was written by brother Amadeus, who signed his name on fol. 109. The two manuscripts are the same size and are laid out and decorated in the same way. Also, the Visconti patronage is repeatedly affirmed by the inclusion of Visconti devices and a profile portrait of Filippo Maria, inserted in the lower margin of fol. 57v of this second volume, corresponds with that of his father, Gian Galeazzo, on fols. 105 and 115 of the first volume. The decoration of this codex was begun at the turn of the fifteenth century, probably between 1399 and 1402, the year that Gian Galeazzo died. Work on the manuscript continued until 1425–1430, with various artists and assistants contributing to the pictorial cycle. The illumination is therefore marked by profound stylistic variations since such a large number of artists were involved in completing the exacting task, all revolving around the workshops of Salomone de' Grassi and Belbello da Pavia.

Fol. 70 shows the murder of Cain by his great-nephew Lamech. According to the *Historia Scolastica* of Peter Comestor (who lived in the second half of the twelfth century), the blind Lamech went out hunting guided by a young man. The boy, however, mistook Cain for some prey and Lamech shot his great-uncle with an arrow; once he realized his error he took his revenge by killing his guide.

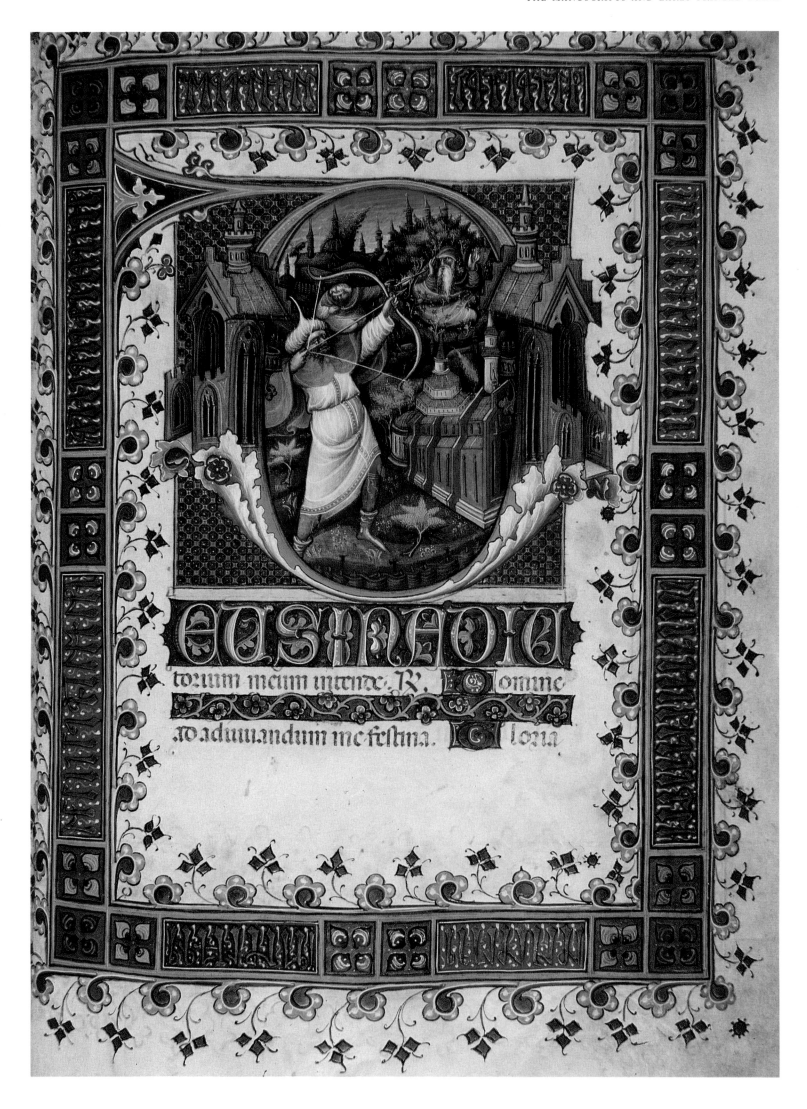

VIRGIL, Eclogues, Georgics, Aeneid

Florence, Biblioteca Medicea Laurenziana

MED. PAL. 69, FOL. 64V

THIS LATIN MANUSCRIPT CONTAINS the three most famous works by Virgil and, as a note on fol. 266v tells us, it was written by Pierre de Lormel d'Alvergne in 1403. We know nothing of this scribe who describes himself in his colophon as '*librarius*' of the University of Paris, and he does not seem to be identifiable with other people of the same name. The volume was commissioned by Jacques Courau, royal councillor and treasurer to Jean de Berry, who commissioned many manuscripts for the Duke.

The text of Virgil is accompanied by marginal and interlinear glosses and by a *Life of the Author*, which is important as evidence of the revival of interest in Virgil and in the study of his work in Paris, where such studies had been neglected since the thirteenth century, with the diffusion of grammatical teaching.

The decoration, which is of the highest quality, includes two miniatures at the beginning of the *Georgics* and the *Aeneid* (fol. 64v); the scene illustrating the *Eclogues* has been removed. The first miniature is attributed to a French illuminator known as the 'Virgil Master', who is documented between the 1390s and 1420s. His consistent narrative style – characterized by wavy, fluctuating drawing and colours applied with delicate brush strokes through which the underdrawing can be seen – can be clearly observed in the scene at the beginning of the *Georgics*. The other miniature, illustrating the journey of Aeneas to Italy, has been attributed to one of his assistants.

GRADUAL

Florence, Biblioteca Medicea Laurenziana

CORALE 3, FOLS. 15, 1V

THIS LARGE CHOIR BOOK (670 x 480 mm), entitled '*Diurno domenicale*' in the incipit, contains the noted chants for the masses from Easter Sunday to the Sunday before Trinity. Dated 1409 (fol. 3), it is illustrated with twenty miniatures (nine for the Sunday masses and eleven for the weekday masses), executed by various artists: Niccolò Rosselli, Zanobi Strozzi, Lorenzo Monaco, Matteo Torelli and Bartolomeo di Fruosino.

Zanobi Strozzi executed the figure of Christ calling the blessed in the initial on fol. 15. Fol. 1v, with the beginning of the Mass for Easter, is framed on four sides by a rich border. The Resurrection is represented at the centre in the letter 'R'; Christ is depicted above ascending to heaven and below the empty tomb is shown, with three sleeping guards. Recent criticism has conflicting views on the attribution of the miniature: some scholars consider it is the work of Niccolò Rosselli, others that it was executed by Lorenzo Monaco and Matteo Torelli. This manuscript (Corale 3) belongs to a group of eighteen choir books which were produced between 1371 and 1420 for the monastery of Santa Maria degli Angeli in Florence. The volumes comprise antiphoners, that is chants and music for the liturgical offices, and graduals, that is chants for the Mass.

In the fifteenth century, the Camaldolese monastery of Santa Maria degli Angeli, founded in 1021, was an important meeting place for artists and humanists. Taddeo Gaddi, Lorenzo Ghiberti, Fra Angelico, Filippo Brunelleschi and other renowned artists worked at the monastery; ancient texts were translated there, and Ambrogio Traversari taught Greek and Latin. The monastery is, however, renowned above all for the production of choir books. These books were so famed in Venice, Rome and even outside Italy, that in the sixteenth century Pope Leo X wanted to take them to Rome. The monks succeeded in keeping the precious volumes until the time of the Napoleonic invasion. At that period many illuminated leaves were cut out from them (three have been taken from this volume), and some whole manuscripts were dismembered and lost. Many of the lost leaves from these volumes have been rediscovered in public and private collections.

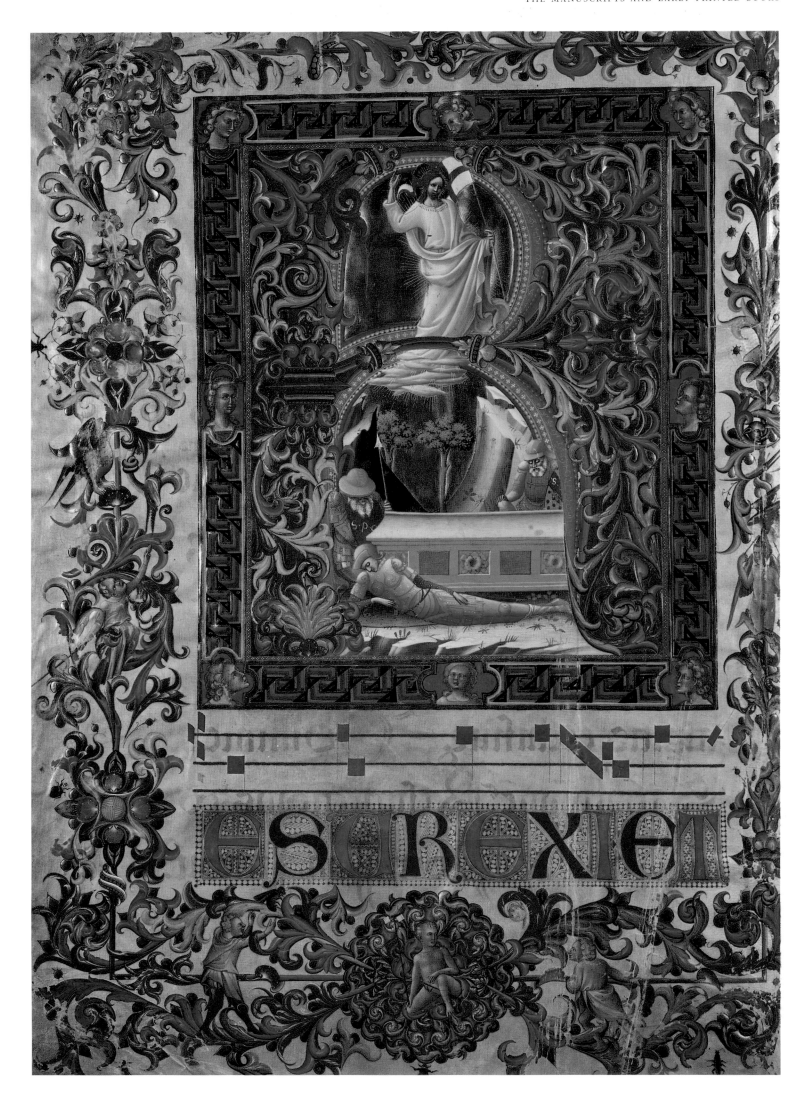

INITIAL N

Milan, Biblioteca Trivulziana

PERGAMENE SCIOLTE, FOL. 12

THIS CUTTING HAS A LARGE INITIAL 'N', which lacks part of its upper decoration. On the verso there are traces of musical notation and writing.

The Presentation of the Virgin at the Temple is depicted within the initial. Joachim and Anna are shown on the left accompanying Mary with loving gestures up the stairs leading to the temple door, from which two priests are welcoming them.

The initial has been attributed to Tomasino da Vimercate, a Lombard artist who was active between 1380/1390 and 1414 and was influenced by Giovannino de' Grassi. Typical of Tomasino's style are the use of bright colours and the careful execution of well-characterized and lively figures, together with a marked taste for decoration. The miniature of the Biblioteca Trivulziana is thought to be one of this illuminator's latest works; other works by the same artist include three books of Hours: one in Modena, one in The Hague produced for Isabella of Castile, and one in the Biblioteca Palatina in Parma.

BOOK OF HOURS

Milan, Biblioteca Trivulziana

2164, FOLS. 2, 6, 188, 192

THIS CODEX IS TYPICALLY FRENCH both in its style of script, in the saints listed in the calendar (those venerated in the Paris region predominate), and in its beautiful decoration.

The manuscript begins with a calendar written in French, with each month on a separate leaf. The lines are written alternately in red and blue ink, with the headings, initials and feast days in gold. The decorative scheme in the calendar consists of two tiny framed pictures on each recto (the leaves measure only 170 x 120 mm) in the outer margins; the upper ones show the occupations of the months, domestic or rural scenes, while the lower ones have a sign of the zodiac for the corresponding month; in the lower margins are pairs of figures representing an Old Testament patriarch and a New Testament saint.

The first two leaves shown are from the calendar for the months of February and June. The following two (the whole cycle of saints includes thirty-two almost full-page miniatures) have miniatures set within arched frames, and show the archangel Saint Michael slaying the devil, against a background of a small island in a sea ploughed by ships, and the stoning of Saint Stephen. Saint Stephen also appears, teaching a small group of people, in the small scene in the lower margin.

Almost all the leaves are framed by elegant borders with flowers, fruit, birds and butterflies, painted in bright colours together with more opaque tones. The garments worn by the figures, often enriched by gold decoration, are executed with remarkable attention to detail.

The codex, is datable to the first half of the fifteenth century (circa 1430–1440) and is a product of the workshop of the 'Bedford Master', a famous Parisian illuminator so-named because three of the works attributed to him were made for John of Lancaster, Duke of Bedford, brother of Henry V.

BIBLE (Bible of Niccolò III d'Este)

Vatican City, Biblioteca Apostolica Vaticana

BARB. LAT. 613, FOL. 514

THIS EXCEPTIONAL MANUSCRIPT, containing the French version of the Bible by Guiard des Moulins, was made for Niccolò III d'Este, Marquis of Ferrara, between 1393 and 1441, the year that he died. The codex is known as the Bible of Niccolò III d'Este or the Belbello Bible since it is richly illuminated by Belbello da Pavia, who is considered to be the last important exponent of the Lombard International Gothic style. He executed a large number of works between about 1422/1425 and 1470.

The decoration of the manuscript consists not only of large miniatures at the beginning of the Old and New Testaments, with rich borders enclosing the two columns of text set in the lower parts of the pages, but also of numerous initials and smaller scenes at the beginning of each book.

The detail shown here depicts the Adoration of the Magi. In this scene one can observe the artist's typical stylistic characteristics: the subtle features of the faces, the well-executed drapery which hangs in sinuous folds, and the monumental scale of the figures.

Belbello must have ceased working on the manuscript by 1434, when Niccolò III commissioned Jacopino d'Arezzo to provide decoration, which was found to be lacking, for the second book of Ezra (fols. 281–289).

ANDREA BIANCO, Nautical Atlas

Venice, Biblioteca Marciana

It. Z. 76 (= 4783), FOL. 10

THIS MANUSCRIPT, one of the most important geographical codices, is dated 1436 and signed by the Venetian cartographer Andrea Bianco.

Besides the wind-roses and six nautical maps, there are two planispheres: that on fol. 10 is a circular planisphere with north to the left. The seas, coloured green (the Mediterranean Sea and Indian Ocean occupy areas of almost equal size), surround the continents: Europe, Asia and Africa.

To the east, that is at the top of the planisphere, the Earthly Paradise is depicted; from it originate four important rivers: the Tigris, Euphrates, Nile and Ganges. Jerusalem is at the centre. The western coasts, those best-known at the time, are drawn with some precision, while the African continent is overly elongated to the west.

It is interesting to note that places are indicated not only by name, but also by drawings and brief captions referring to ancient medieval legends.

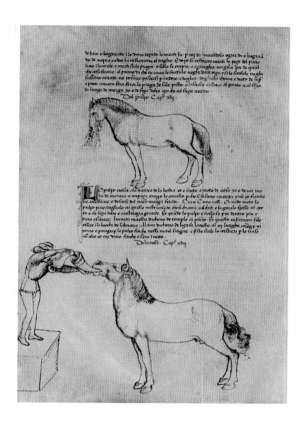

BONIFACIO DI CALABRIA, Mascalcia

Modena, Biblioteca Estense

It. 464 (= α. J. 3. 13), fols. 6v, 52

THE MANUSCRIPT CONTAINS a treatise concerning horses, their illnesses and the cures for them, and is one of the earliest works on this subject. It is illustrated by fifteen drawings of horses and grooms: some are executed in pen, while others are merely outlined in silver point. The drawings show horses in both health and sickness and the cures that grooms can administer to them. Ninety-two drawings of bits and harnesses of various types are added in the last part of the codex.

The style of the pen drawings, which are carefully executed, suggests that the manuscript was produced in the Veneto-Lombard region in the first half of the fifteenth century, but the group of ninety-two drawings was added at a later date.

The manuscript appears as number nine in the inventory of the Ducal Library of Ferrara compiled in 1467 on the orders of Borso d'Este.

A chauallo polledro che gitta la ligua ple cinelle.

A chauallo polledro no scalgionato.

A chauallo de schanecça.

A chauallo che ua troppo in sula schena.

A chauallo che prieme piu da luna mano cha dalaltra.

A chauallo che tre di chalci.

A chauallo che tira troppo la mano.

A chauallo che a piccola bocha.

A chauallo che alça troppo el capo.

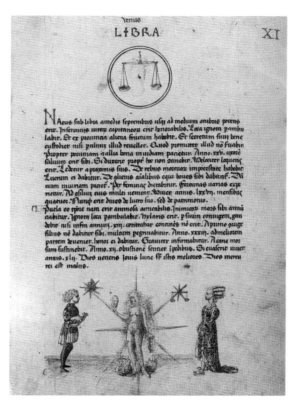

LIBER PHYSIOGNOMIAE

Modena, Biblioteca Estense

LAT. 696 (= α. W. 8. 20), FOLS. 1, 6, 3-8V

THE MANUSCRIPT BEGINS WITH HOROSCOPES of people born under the twelve signs of the zodiac, and an account of the characteristics of men and women influenced by the various constellations. This first part is followed by an actual astrological and astronomical treatise, dealing with the planets, months and days.

The decoration, which can be dated between 1440 and 1450 on stylistic grounds, is laid out on twelve pages, each devoted to a sign and illustrated with watercolour drawings of the symbols of the zodiac; in the lower part of each page the planets are represented in human form, as well as the activities and temperaments favoured by the different astral conjunctions. A good example is fol. 6, representing Libra. At the top, in red ink, are the name of the planet and the sign with the constellation itself represented within a circle. In the bottom margin, below the text, Venus is shown naked in the centre, standing on a fire; on either side of her are, above, the signs of Libra and Taurus and, below, a young man playing the mandolin and a girl wearing an elegant brocade dress.

On the facing page here are reproduced all the signs of the zodiac from fols. 3–8v.

The unidentified artist was influenced by Pisanello and was probably active in the courts of the Po valley (Mantua, Ferrara, Verona), although he clearly also knew Paduan work.

Mars
ARIES

Venus
LIBRA

Venus
TAVRVS

Mars
SCORPIVS

Mercurius
GEMINI

Jouis
SAGITARIVS

Luna
CANCER

Saturno
CAPRICORNIVS

Sol
LEO

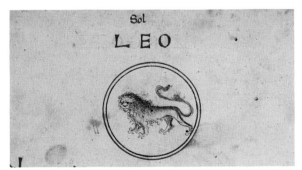

Saturno
AQVARIVS

Mercurius
VIRGO

Jouis
PISSES

CICERO, Pro Marcello, De Senectute

Milan, Biblioteca Trivulziana

693, FOL. 33

T HE MANUSCRIPT CONTAINS two works by Cicero: the oration *Pro Marcello*, and the philosophical text *De Senectute*, together with the French version of the latter made by Laurent de Premierfait. He was secretary to Jean de Berry and one of the most important French humanists, and was killed in 1418 by the Burgundians during the taking of Paris. His translation of *De Senectute* was completed in 1405 (the date is in fact included in the explicit of the manuscript on fol. 105) and was dedicated to Louis II, Duke of Bourbon (1356–1410). In 1409 Premierfait also made a translation of Boccaccio's *De casibus virorum illustrium*, which enjoyed enormous success, and in 1414 he translated the *Decameron*; both volumes are dedicated to Jean de Berry.

On fol. 33 of the manuscript, Laurent de Premierfait is shown presenting the work to Louis, Duke of Bourbon. Scholarly opinion is divided as to the authorship of the miniature and the date of its execution. The manuscript is thought by some to be the dedication copy to the Duke of Bourbon because of the coat of arms with fleurs-de-lis but other critics do not consider the coat of arms and other decorative borders to be original.

Comparison with other manuscripts of similar style and with similar decorative motifs has suggested the existence of an illuminator known as the 'Master of the Paris Bartholomaeus Anglicus', whose style differed from contemporary artistic currents and was linked to that of the preceding generation, although he stresses colour and expressive qualities in the figures.

Analysis of stylistic features has made it possible to date the manuscript between 1445 and 1450 and to localize it in the region of Le Mans.

t resexcellant tglorieux et noble
prince. loys oncle de roy de frace
duc de bourbon conte de clermot
et de forestz. seigneur de beauseu
trant chamberier et per de france. droictemet
et bien vser de lostre dignite et puissance ~
terrienne victoire desure de tous voz ennemis
manifestes et cachiez. accroissement de bon
nes meurs et vertuz. et entier accomplisse
ment de lostre bonne esperance. Et a lous
comme seigneur et prince. prompte et

TELESFORO DA COSENZA,
Liber de causis, de statu, cognitione ac fine presentis et tribulationum futurarum

Modena, Biblioteca Estense

LAT. 233 (= α. M. 5. 27), FOLS. 47, 39V

THE PROPHECIES OF TELESFORO OF COSENZA are followed by the *Vaticinia Pontificum*, attributed to Joachim of Fiore. These two texts, which enjoyed particular popularity in the fifteenth century, described the suffering humanity would endure if it abandoned the teachings of the pope, and as such they were well received by the papal authorities.

This manuscript was commissioned by Leonello d'Este (whose illuminated coat of arms is on fol. 12) in 1445 or 1446. It had already been copied by 1447, since the last pope present in the list is Eugenius IV, who died in that year. The decoration of fol. 12, a border of vine leaves and bunches of grapes on a gold ground, was executed at the same time and is attributed to the Ferrarese school. The series of watercolour illustrations which complete the codex was executed at a later date. They were originally attributed to Bonifacio Bembo, a Paduan illuminator and painter, but recent criticism considers them to have been executed in Emilia for stylistic reasons.

The first scene shown here (fol. 47) represents the pope seated on a throne between two pilgrims, with clerics and laymen seated before him on low benches and seen from behind. The other illustration (fol. 39v) depicts a regal procession: three mounted sovereigns in the centre are preceded and followed by horsemen in armour.

MISSAL (Missal of Borso d'Este)

Modena, Biblioteca Estense

LAT. 239 (= α. W. 5. 2), FOL. 7

THIS MANUSCRIPT, one of the most interesting examples of Ferrarese illumination of the Renaissance, is generally known as the Missal of Borso d'Este.

From documentary evidence we learn that the manuscript was begun in 1449 for Leonello d'Este and completed eight years later, in 1457, for his brother Borso. In the past, most critics attributed the decoration to Taddeo Crivelli; in reality it was executed by Giorgio d'Alemagna, one of the greatest Ferrarese illuminators of the fifteenth century, with the help of many assistants.

The attribution to Giorgio d'Alemagna, supported by documentary evidence (his activity at the Este court, first under Leonello and later under Borso, is widely documented), has produced new evidence for the working practices of this artist; analysis of the decoration of this manuscript has shown that it was not executed following the order of the quires.

Three of the 314 leaves are illuminated with scenes and borders, and there are also ninety-eight decorated initials, and thirty-nine historiated initials. The miniature reproduced here shows a rocky landscape out of which emerges a purple, church-like building and red embattled towers set beneath a soft blue sky studded with gold clouds. The side of the building consists of a portico, supported by fluted columns and pilasters, under which David kneels, attacked by demons. To the left of the scene, a seated prophet is writing on a scroll. David is also represented in the historiated initial below.

The manuscript is still in its original binding, covered in purple velvet, with rectangular panels of braid on the silver-gilt boards. The corner pieces and central bosses, with the Este coat of arms, were possibly executed by Amadio da Milano.

SILIUS ITALICUS, De bello punico

Venice, Biblioteca Marciana

LAT. XII. 68 (= 4519), FOL. 3, DETACHED LEAF

IN THE SECOND EDITION of his *Lives*, Giorgio Vasari describes this magnificent Florentine codex, which had been seen by Cosimo Bartoli in the Dominican convent of SS. Giovanni e Paolo in Venice. According to Vasari's source, the decoration was made up of 'small pictures' representing Silius Italicus, Scipio Africanus, Hannibal, Nicholas V, Mars, Neptune and Rome; he describes each in detail and attributes them to Attavante.

It is thought that the miniatures were removed from the manuscript in the eighteenth century, when it was still in the convent library. Today the only important leaf that remains in the codex is fol. 3 (the first), which is attributed to Zanobi Strozzi. It is the frontispiece to the text, decorated with a sumptuous border of white vine scrolling, framing warriors, putti and animals set within a continuous series of medallions. In the initial a crowned *condottiere* is set against a landscape of hills and cypresses; a caption describes the figure as '*Silius auctor*'.

Of the leaves that were removed, one was recovered by Giovanni Maria Sasso and donated to the Biblioteca Marciana so that it could be reunited with the manuscript. It shows Mars on a two-wheeled chariot and is considered to be the work of Francesco Pesellino, who was active from 1447 to 1455; he is thought to have executed the other miniatures that are now lost.

The manuscript is datable to the mid-fifteenth century and is thought to have been made for Pope Nicholas V, whose portrait was on one of the lost leaves. This attractive hypothesis is not supported by Vespasiano da Bisticci's *Life of Nicholas V*, although it is convincing in terms of the Pope's character and humanist interests.

GILIO DE' ZELATI DI FAENZA,
Partiti de gioco de scachi
(Chess games)

Turin, Biblioteca Reale

VARIA 128, FOL. 11

THIS MANUSCRIPT IS OF INTEREST for the light it sheds on the game of chess in the fifteenth century. The work, the title of which is taken from the preface, was dedicated by the author to Borso d'Este, the Duke of Ferrara.

The preface, written in Italian, is followed by twenty-three illustrations, each of which is devoted to a game. Six of the illustrations appear to have been designed by the author himself.

On the recto of each leaf there is a chess board drawn in red ink. It consists of a 12 cm square divided into smaller squares. The pieces are shown in the squares, with the white pieces painted in red and the black in green. Each piece is given its Latin name, and letters of the alphabet show the moves to be executed; several errors in the placing of pieces have been corrected with the word 'vacat', to indicate that the square should be empty. The text explaining each game is set out on the versos, facing the illustrations.

The coat of arms painted in the manuscript, showing an eagle surmounted by a crown, shows that the manuscript was made for the Este family library.

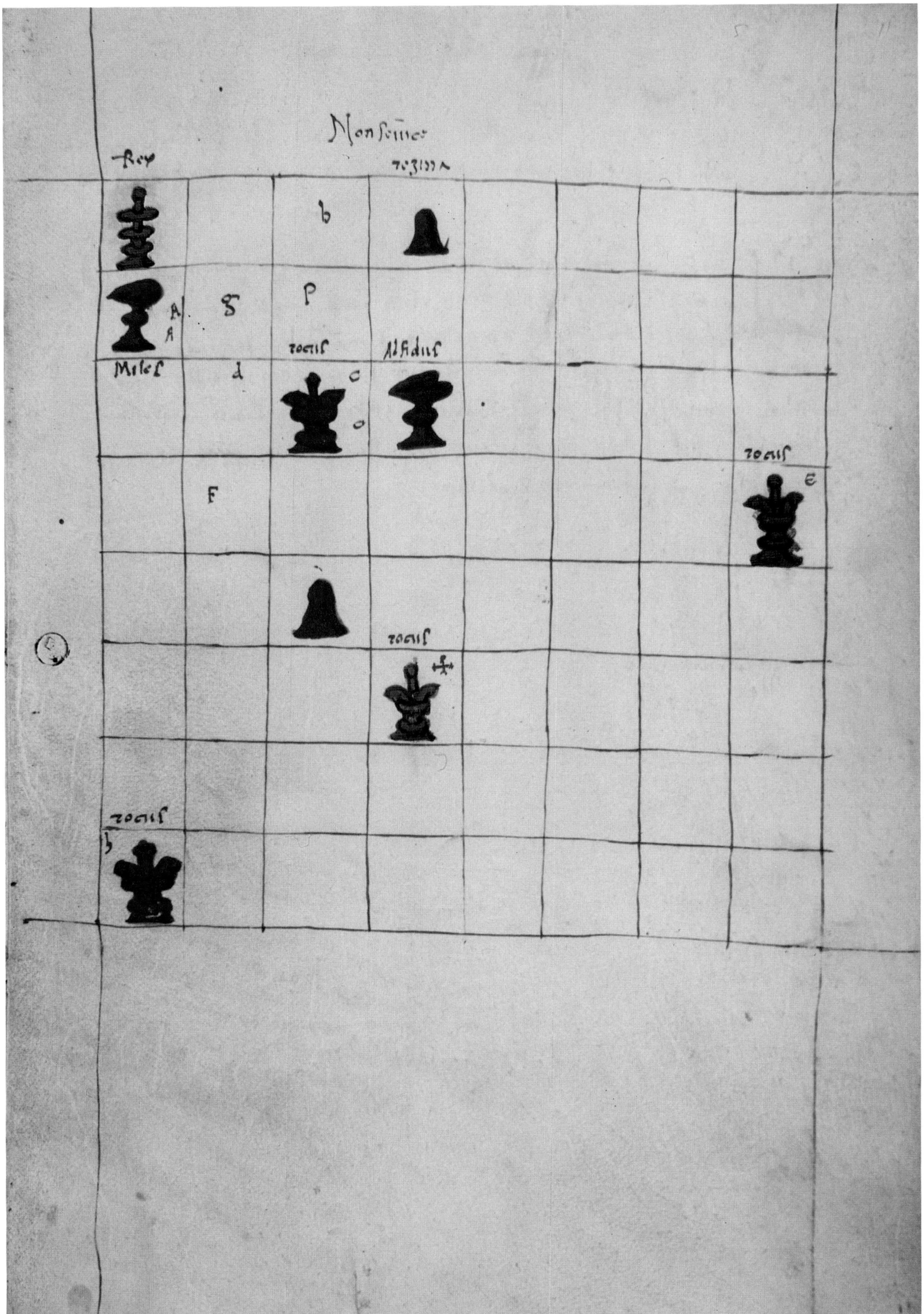
Monseñor
Rey
Reyna
Miles
Alfidus
rocus
rocus
rocus
rocus

LIBER DE SIMPLICIBUS

Venice, Biblioteca Marciana

LAT. VI. 59 (= 2548), FOL. 328

THIS FINE CODEX IS A HERBAL; the text is thought to have been composed by Niccolò Roccabonella of Conegliano, a doctor who practiced in Venice from 1415 to 1448 and in Zara from 1449 to 1453. In Zara he came in contact with Johann Reinhardt, a German druggist who probably provided the German and Czech names in the text.

The decoration is the work of Andrea Amadio, a painter about whom virtually nothing is known. Some of the fine illustrations were drawn directly from specimens, others derive from the typical repertories of many Herbals, which were based on the drawings in the work of Dioscorides, and still others are based on another codex of the same type, the Carrara Herbal, datable to between the end of the fourteenth and the beginning of the fifteenth century and now in London.

The manuscript belonged to Benedetto Rin (1485–1565) and his descendants, owners of a pharmacy near the Rialto Bridge in Venice. In 1604 the family donated it to the Dominican monks of the church of SS. Giovanni e Paolo, on condition that it was carefully looked after.

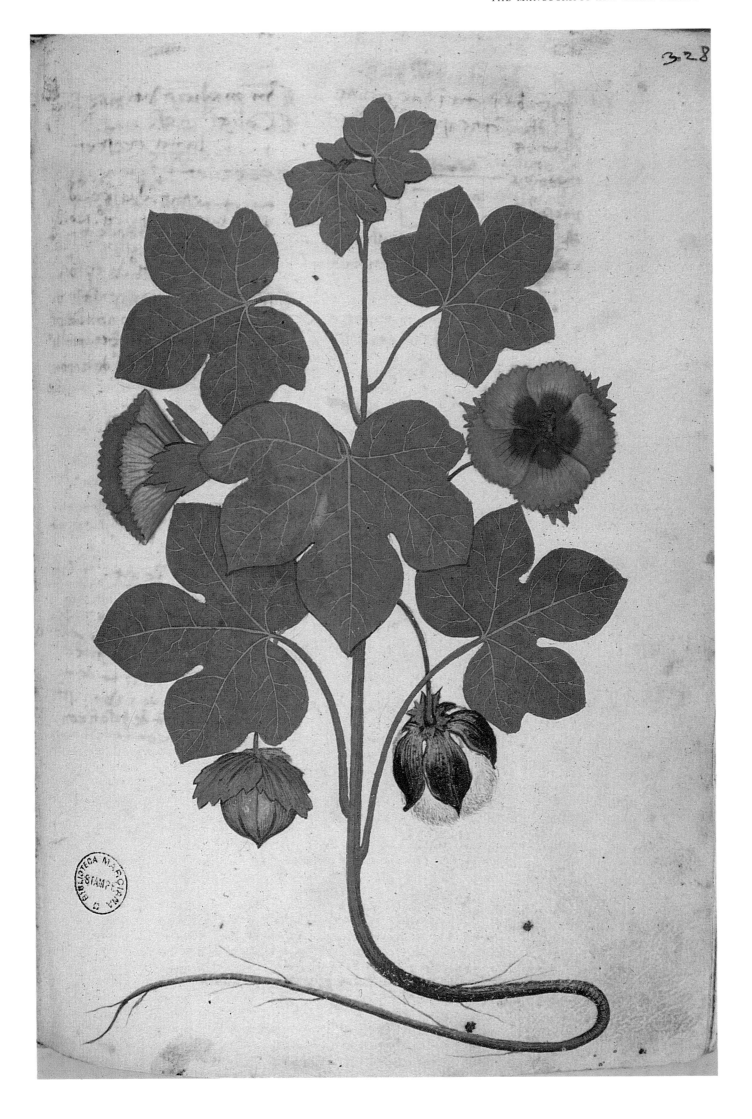

PETRARCH,
Canzoniere and Trionfi

Florence, Biblioteca Nazionale Centrale

PAL. 192, FOLS. 1, 43

THIS TYPICAL FLORENTINE RENAISSANCE CODEX contains the
Trionfi followed by the sonnets of the *Canzoniere*. The opening
pages of the *Trionfi* are each decorated with a wide border of white
vine scroll inhabited by multicoloured birds and with a rectangular
miniature, which occupies the upper part of the page and extends
into the outer margin, interrupting the border decoration. The
opening page of the *Canzoniere* has a similar miniature with white
vine decoration inhabited by animals and putti and with a coat of
arms within a laurel wreath; the motifs on the arms have been
totally erased so that it is not possible to identify the original
owner of the manuscript.

The codex was copied by an anonymous scribe to whom a
further two manuscripts in Italian and nine in Latin have been
attributed; he was active from the second decade of the fifteenth
century. The decoration of the *Trionfi* is attributed to Giovanni
Varnucci. It belongs to Varnucci's late period, between 1450 and
1457, and can be seen as a delightful forerunner to the famous
series of manuscripts of the *Trionfi* illuminated by Francesco
d'Antonio del Chierico. The scene on fol. 1 represents the Triumph
of Love and that on fol. 43 shows the Triumph of Time. The
figures are painted with great care, with their ages and social ranks
well characterized; they are valuable for the evidence that they provide for the study of costume in this period. The wide landscapes
are influenced by Domenico Veneziano.

43

DE SPHAERA

Modena, Biblioteca Estense

LAT. 209 (= α. X. 2. 14), FOLS. 10V-11, 6V

T HE MANUSCRIPT CONSISTS of a few richly decorated leaves. The first three have pen drawings representing the elements, the movement of the planets, eclipses, climates, the constellations and the phases of the moon. The emblems and coats of arms of Francesco Sforza and his wife Bianca Maria Visconti are depicted on fol. 4. Full-page miniatures follow, showing the seven planets in human form and, on the facing pages, the influences that each exercises on human activities. On fol. 10v Mercury is shown holding the bag and caduceus, symbols respectively of wealth and prosperity in times of peace; the zodiac signs of Gemini and Virgo are depicted in medallions. The facing page represents activities benignly influenced by Mercury.

On fol. 6v Jupiter is depicted, within concentric, iridescent circles, holding the sceptre in his left hand, arrows in his right and the quiver slung over his shoulder. The two medallions at his feet contain the zodiac signs of Pisces and Sagittarius. The scene below represents the three shops of a fruit seller, a grain seller and a banker.

The exquisite decoration of this manuscript has been attributed to Cristoforo de' Predis, a Lombard artist born in the first forty years of the fifteenth century, but the style appears closer to that of the 'Master of Ippolita Sforza'. Although the style of the decoration suggests that the manuscript was produced between 1450 and 1460, it has not yet proved possible to identify the author of the text, which merely consists of a few lines of verse explaining each of the pictures. It has been suggested that the artist drew on the astrological work of John of Sacrobosco and that Francesco Filelfo collaborated in writing the text.

·IVPITER·

Benegno e ioue e de uirtu pianeta
Produce mathematici e doctori
Theologi et gransauij ne diueta
Alchuna gentil cosa o grandi honori

PSALTER, SMALL OFFICES, OFFICE OF THE BLESSED VIRGIN

Milan, Biblioteca Trivulziana

448, FOL. 76

THE MANUSCRIPT HAS NINETEEN LEAVES WITH MINIATURES, enclosed by arched frames surrounded with borders of foliate motifs, and accompanied by a decorated initial introducing the text. On fol. 76 David is shown with a fool before him dressed as a jester.

According to notes written by don Carlo Trivulzio on the flyleaf, the manuscript was executed in France after 1450, since Saint Bernardino of Siena, who was canonized in that year, is included in the calendar. Scholars have also drawn attention to the inclusion in red in the calendar of Saint Nicasius (14 December), the Bishop of Rheims, and have concluded that the manuscript was produced by the Franco-Flemish school.

The naturalistic external backgrounds to the figures are marked by a recurrent use of green and the inclusion of rivers and windmills; the carefully depicted interiors show mosaic floors and pink grounds decorated with gilt sprays. The figure drawing, which shows a certain liveliness and taste for detail in the depiction of settings, is not as finely executed as the borders framing the pages.

The origin of the codex remains uncertain, although stylistic features might suggest the Duchy of Savoy. There are, however, typically Flemish elements which recall the work of the artist known as the 'Gold Scrolls Master' and of Willelm Vrelant.

BOOK OF HOURS

Naples, Biblioteca Vittorio Emanuele III

I. B. 30, FOL. 94

THE BOOK OF HOURS, a fundamental text for private prayer, enjoyed widespread popularity in north-central Europe, particularly in France and in the Low Countries.

The present manuscript, written in French gothic script, is decorated in the margins of the folios containing the calendar with elegant borders of polychrome leaves and flowers, interspersed with birds and butterflies. Similar borders, in which the whole range of tones are employed, from azure to blue, pink to purple, as well as gold and the essential green, form the backdrop for fifteen miniatures, enclosed by arched frames, all but one representing episodes from the life of Christ. The exception is the scene of David and Bathsheba shown here, the only Old Testament episode included in the decorative scheme. The story narrates how this exceptionally beautiful Israelite woman became David's paramour after he killed her husband. David, reproved by the prophet Nathan and threatened with divine retribution, repented and composed the famous Psalm *Miserere.* The miniature shows David playing the lyre and Bathsheba bathing; the small scene above shows David's repentance.

The treatment of the miniatures in the manuscript is somewhat unequal, at times even coarse, yet the scenes express a marked taste for narrative and are also detailed depictions of everyday life. The manuscript is typical of the Franco-Burgundian school of the beginning of the second half of the fifteenth century, which was heavily influenced by Flemish styles.

AVICENNA,
Canon medicinae

Florence, Biblioteca Medicea Laurenziana

GADDI 24, FOL. 1

AVICENNA, A MUSLIM PHILOSOPHER, doctor, scientist and poet, lived from 980 to 1037. The most important of his medical works is the *Canon medicinae*, which was translated into Latin by Gerard of Cremona and was one of the texts most studied at European universities. The work is divided into five sections: the first concerns general medicine and anatomy, the second deals with medication, the third outlines the diseases of particular parts of the body, the fourth addresses illnesses in general, and the fifth describes the composition and application of medication.

This manuscript contains only the first two and the fourth sections; it was made for Sozino Benzi, the doctor of Pope Pius II. The detail of fol. 1 shows one of the most beautiful examples of fifteenth-century Ferrarese illumination; it is attributed to Matteo Crivelli, who was active between 1452 and 1476. The scene shows Avicenna, the author of the work, seated at a table before his patients. The other miniatures in the manuscript were executed by an artist known as 'Pseudo-Michele da Carrara', whose activity is documented in Rome around 1463.

PTOLEMY, Geography

Venice, Biblioteca Marciana

GR. Z. 388 (= 333), FOL. VI V

THE MANUSCRIPT IS ONE of the de luxe copies of Ptolemy's *Geography* which belonged to Cardinal Bessarion, whose library was so important in the fifteenth century that it was considered the finest Greek library in the world, superior even to that of the popes. The Greek manuscripts in the library are extremely valuable since they contain the oldest or best version of each work and offer a complete panorama of every field of Greek culture.

This manuscript of Ptolemy's *Geography* was transcribed by John Rhosus, one of the most active Greek scribes of the fifteenth century, who copied over twenty codices for Bessarion. Cardinal Bessarion certainly commissioned the present work for he wrote his *ex-libris* in Greek and Latin on fol. IV and his coat of arms, supported by a putto, is painted in the lower margin of the first page of the text, set in a frame of white vine scrolling.

As is usual in manuscripts of Ptolemy, the text is furnished with a map of the world, which is richly decorated with representations of the winds and the signs of the zodiac. It is followed by twenty-six further maps of inferior execution. The last of the flyleaves preceding the text (fol. VIv) is occupied by a large miniature set within an elegant frame of red and blue volutes. It shows Ptolemy, wearing a crown and a rich brocade garment bordered with ermine, as he takes measurements with an astrolabe. On the right is a study containing another astrolabe, various astronomical instruments and numerous books, including an open atlas. In the background is an imposing structure with gothicised architecture in bright colours, which is reminiscent of Venetian buildings. In the lower margin of the same page is a Greek epigram in praise of Ptolemy, translated into Latin for Bessarion by his secretary Niccolò Perotti, which makes it possible to date the codex to approximately 1453. The decoration on fol. IV and the initials are by a Florentine hand or hands, but the portrait of Ptolemy appears to have been executed in Bologna, where Bessarion was papal legate in the early 1450s.

Ἐπίγραμμα ὅπ ἐξάπε πτολεμαῖ εἰς ἑαυτόν

ΟΙΑΟΤΙ ΘΝΗΤΟС ΕΦΥΝ ΚΑΙ ΕΦΗΜΕΡΟС, ΑΛΛΟΤΑΝ ΑСΤΡΩΝ
ΜΑСΤΕΥΩ, ΠΥΚΝΑС ΑΜΦΙΔΡΟΜΟΥС ΕΛΙΚΑС
ΟΥΚΕΤΕΠΙΨΑΥΩ ΓΑΙΗС ΠΟСΙΝ, ΑΛΛΑ ΠΑΡΑΥΤΩ
ΖΗΝΙ, ΘΕΟΤΡΟΦΕΟС ΠΙΜΠΛΑΜΑΙ ΑΜΒΡΟСΙΗС

EPIGRĀMA PTOLEMEI.
MORTALEM VITAM PERITVRA Q₃ MEMBRA DEDERE
FATA MIHI, & SVMVM PRESTITVERE DIEM.
SED IOVIS AMBROSIA VESCOR, TERRAM Q₃ RELINQVO.
INGENIO CVRSVS DVM NOTO SYDEREOS.

GIOVANNI MICHELE ALBERTO CARRARA, Armiranda

Milan, Biblioteca Trivulziana

763, FOL. 1V

THE MANUSCRIPT CONTAINS A COMEDY in Latin by the humanist Giovanni Michele Alberto da Carrara from Bergamo (1438–1490), followed by several Latin verses composed in 1457. The beautiful scene which serves as a frontispiece shows two figures standing in a circular flower meadow, surrounded by a woven wicker fence, set against a white ground studded with gold rosettes. On the left, the author, wearing black and purple, is shown offering his work to the woman standing in front of him who wears an elegant red brocade garment with gold decoration and ermine trimmings. She is shown offering a laurel crown to the author and can thus be identified as Fame. The elegant decoration, which is marked by a judicious use of colour, was executed at the same time as the manuscript, which is dated 1457 in the text.

Some stylistic characteristics, such as the pointed profiles of the two figures, the long fingers of the hands and the carpet of grass covered with yellow veined leaves can be compared with elements in works by Bonifacio Bembo, to whom this miniature can also be attributed.

TRACTATUS DE HERBIS

Modena, Biblioteca Estense

LAT. 993 (= α. L. 9. 28), FOLS. 50, 92

THIS MANUSCRIPT CONTAINING the work of Plateario and Bartolomeo Mini, is considered to be one of the most important Herbals in the Biblioteca Estense. It consists of 168 leaves, with the text written in two columns of forty-two lines.

The very rich illustration, with twenty-two small miniatures, 390 illustrations of herbs and plants, five of animals, and fifty of minerals and medicinal woods, is attributed to an illuminator known as the 'Master of the Prince of Piedmont'. The artist also decorated two books of Hours with the arms of the House of Savoy: MS. HB.I.175 in the Württembergische Landesbibliothek in Stuttgart (which bears the coat of arms of the Prince of Piedmont, the title taken by Amedeo IX between 1439 and 1465, the year he was nominated Duke), and MS. 115 in the Bibliothèque de l'Arsenal in Paris. The provincial and highly narrative style associated with a developed taste for colour have led critics to assume that the artist was active not at the Court of Savoy, but in an area bordering Savoy, namely Bresse, which is where the future Duke Amedeo IX lived. The decoration of the manuscript in the Biblioteca Estense, the only one by this artist to have a non-religious subject, can be securely attributed to him not only on stylistic grounds, but also on account of the date and place of production: the colophon states that the manuscript was written in 1458 in Bourg en Bresse.

The detail of fol. 92 illustrates the collection of honey; beneath a shelter a woman lifts a hive made from a tree trunk and protects her face with her hand. A brown bear is depicted beneath the table.

duriciem cortex zadices cu dicta herbit
maceretur p xv dies i vino z olo pst
modum fiat decocio postea colet z colate
addatur cera et oleu z fiat vnguentu
optimum contra predictu vicium zc

Del calidum est in primo ctradu
siccum in scdo. Mel artificiose
ex apibus hr. componmitatur dum eu

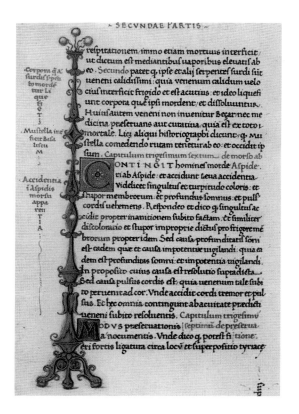

GIOVANNI MATTEO FERRARI,
De evitandis venenis et eorum remediis

Rome, Biblioteca Casanatense

125, FOLS. 50V, 11

GIOVANNI MATTEO FERRARI, who was born in Grado towards the end of the fourteenth century and died in about 1470, was a doctor in Milan before he became a teacher in Pavia and the court doctor of Francesco Sforza. He was considered a great diagnostician and emphasized the importance of anatomical studies in practical medicine. His most famous work, *Practica vel commentarius textualis in IX Rhazis ad Almansorem*, is a commentary on the text by the Persian doctor Rasis, enriched with many personal observations.

The present work, containing a treatise on poisons and their remedies, was dedicated by the author to Francesco Sforza, the Duke of Milan, as can be seen from the preface on fol. 11, but this is not the dedication copy. The present manuscript was copied in Naples and signed by the prolific scribe Giovanni Marco Cinico of Parma. He was a pupil of the Florentine scribe Piero Strozzi and worked at the court of Naples from 1458 to 1498.

Fol. 11 is finely decorated with festoons of laurel interspersed with cameos and pearls. There are portraits of four Roman emperors in the corners: Octavian, Titus, Nero and Domitian. The initial letter is suspended in an original manner from the frame. In the background to it there is a unicorn in front of a sheet of water in which aquatic reptiles swim, set against a peaceful landscape. The finely executed illumination shows a particularly bright range of colours and a taste for ornamentation which reflect the influence of the 'Paduan-Roman' style. The artist is identifiable as Giovanni Todeschino, who also worked for the court in Naples and is named as '*miniatore del senyor Rey*' (illuminator of the lord King) in payments between 1487 and 1492. He decorated a copy of the *Decades* of Flavio Biondo now in Munich (Bayerische Staatsbibliothek, clm. 11324), which was copied for King Alfonso II in 1494, and also a Horace in Berlin (Kupferstichkabinett, 78 D 14), which has the Royal Arms of Naples and was probably also made for Alfonso II (1494–1495).

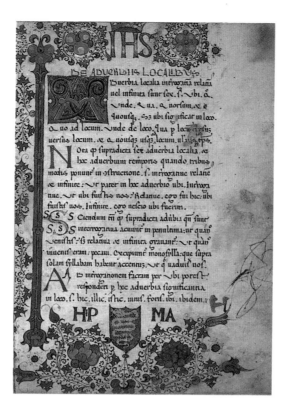

BALDO MARTORELLI,
Grammar

Milan, Biblioteca Trivulziana

786, FOL. 1, DETACHED LEAF

THIS SMALL MANUSCRIPT, datable to between 1454 and 1460, contains a grammatical text which was compiled for Ippolita, the daughter of Francesco Sforza, Duke of Milan, and Bianca Maria Visconti. The decoration consists of initials and a frontispiece bearing the coat of arms and initials 'HIP MA' of Ippolita Maria for whom it was intended.

A leaf with a portrait of Duke Francesco, which was executed at the same period, was added to the manuscript at a later date. There are other extant portraits of Francesco, but their different stylistic features make it impossible to compare them to the example in this manuscript. The closest is the portrait in MS. Varia 75 of the Biblioteca Reale in Turin. It is not by the same hand, but it shows affinities to this portrait which indicate that it came from the same cultural circle. Although the portrait shown here is not considered to be by the hand of any of the illuminators active in the 1460s, it can certainly be attributed to the Lombard school, perhaps to one of the painters active in the time of Francesco.

ROBERTO DELLA PORTA, Romuleon

Florence, Biblioteca Medicea Laurenziana

MED. PAL. 156. 1, FOL. 1; MED. PAL. 156. 2, FOL. 215

THE WORK CONTAINED in these two manuscripts is a compendium of Roman history from the foundation of the city to the age of Constantine. It was composed in the fourteenth century by the Bolognese author Roberto della Porta for Gomez Albornoz, the governor of Bologna, and translated into French for the Duke of Burgundy, Philip the Good, who was one of the greatest bibliophiles of the fifteenth century.

The two manuscripts were produced and copied by David Aubert, originally from Hesdin, who dominated the book market of Bruges from 1460. His workshop produced numerous manuscripts. Among its illuminators was Loyset Liédet, also from Hesdin, who executed the miniatures shown here. On fol. 1 of the first volume, on the right, Philip the Good and other members of the court are shown visiting David Aubert's shop. The scene on fol. 215 of the second volume shows the entrance of an army into a town.

r commence vng liure Intitule Romu

UNIVERSAL HISTORY (HISTOIRE UNIVERSELLE)

Rome, Biblioteca Casanatense

233, FOL. 171

THE UNIVERSAL HISTORY narrated in this manuscript goes from the creation of man to the war between Caesar and Pompey. It is in French and is illustrated by eleven miniatures; there may originally have been twelve, since there was probably one on the first leaf, which is now missing. Two of the miniatures, which are coloured, are of larger dimensions than the rest, filling the upper half of the pages; the other nine are set in the columns and drawn only in black and white. In the miniature on fol. 171, reproduced here, which shows the burning of Troy, palaces being consumed by flames stand out in the background while ships are foundering at sea and in the foreground a procession of women and children is seen abandoning the city, led by a male figure who presumably represents Aeneas. The miniature is framed by a rich but delicate floral border which fills the side and bottom margins of the page and also intrudes on the space between the columns of text, while the upper margin is occupied by the arched frame which encloses the scene.

The style of the buildings, the types of clothes worn by the figures and the settings of the scenes in the miniatures indicate that the manuscript was produced in France, in the region between Burgundy and Provence. The picturesque setting of the scene on fol. 171, and the refinement of the drawing support its attribution to Loyset Liédet, an outstanding representative of the Flemish school who worked for the dukes of Burgundy between 1460 and 1478 (see p. 174). His most successful work is to be found in scenes which are small in compass; in larger scale images his style tends to be over-formal and his figures become rigid.

us que la cite de
twie fut embrasee
qui vii ans mist
a ardoir. Les chretiens qui leur
nefz auoient appareillies et
chaugiez de lauoir et de riches
se de twie saurent et de filz
se murent en mer pour zaler
en leur contree · mais male
ment leur en aduint · car
encore quilz y semblent fut
moult amendrie leur com
paigne · et vous diray com
ment · Palamedes qui fut
moze en twie fut filz au roy
mamuns qui tenoit la mon

taigne de carhareum qui sur
la mer estoit assise · dessoub;
celle montaigne vers la mer
et dedens auoit rochez qui estoi
ent couuertes daue et telles
y auoit qui apparoient · et
pour ce y estoit la mer milt
perilleuse · Quant le roy ma
mpne qui moult estoit dolat
de son filz qui estoit occiz a twie
seut que les chretiens sen re
tournoient il fist alumer feu
par nuit obsture qui estoit
sur celle montaigne pource
que les chretiens quil moult
haioit y semblent · et ossy firet

PIETRO CANDIDO DECEMBRIO, In libris Epitomarum illustriorum virorum Plutarchi

Verona, Biblioteca Capitolare

CCXXXIX (= 200), FOLS. 88V, 98V, 107, 237

Pietro candido decembrio (1399–1472), a humanist who was started in his studies and political career by his father, worked for Filippo Maria Visconti from 1419 to 1447, and as a secretary at the Aragonese court, with a brief interval as a *magister brevium* at the Papal Curia. He translated many texts from Greek and wrote epigrams and the biographies of Francesco Sforza and Filippo Maria Visconti. He is more famous, however, for his *Epistolario* or letter collection, a document of fundamental importance for the study of the political and literary history of his time.

This manuscript, which consists of three volumes of the *Epitome* of Plutarch (the second and third volumes are incomplete), was copied by Lorenzo Dolabella, who signed his name on fol. 270v. It belonged to Taddeo Fissagra, whose coat of arms was painted over an earlier, erased shield on fol. 4.

From Decembrio's *Epistolario* we learn that the manuscript was sent by Fissagra, the owner, in January 1461 to the humanist so that he could have a copy made from it to send to Sigismondo Malatesta.

The Veronese manuscript, which must therefore have been made before 1461, is decorated with fine miniatures of the Lombard school and contains the most complete fifteenth-century figurative commentary to Plutarch's work.

The four initials shown here represent Cato the Censor, wearing a cloak and a laurel wreath and holding a book in his left hand and a lance with an oriflamme decorated with an eagle in his right; Pyrrhus holding a lance in his left hand and wearing a hat encircled by a crown; Marius, wearing an opulent garment bordered in ermine, and holding a lance similar to that in the first miniature; and finally Pelopides wearing ornate armour and carrying a bow and arrow.

The illumination has been attributed to the 'Master of the Vitae imperatorum', an Olivetan monk active between 1413 and 1459.

pore ob virtutis specamen: qu
et experientia pollent. eos ca

D E PYRRHO EPIROTARE REGE 1
RATIO OCTAVA . EPITOMA . P .

in tutum euasit . Nam cum fug

illius ingenium eius abhorens a
nis: &l suauitas humanitate cor

D E PELOPIDA THEBANO ILLVSTR
SEXTA DECIMA EPITOMA . P . CAN

tulisset. fr cum ex oibs unum dutax
nullo pacto adducere posset. vt eius

RAFFAELE VIMERCATI,
Liber iudiciorum

Milan, Biblioteca Trivulziana

1329, FOL. 1

THE MANUSCRIPT, which was completed in 1461 as we learn from the colophon, contains the horoscope that the author, Raffaele Vimercati, made for Galeazzo Maria Sforza, the future Duke of Milan. The only miniature in the codex, on fol. 1, is bordered on the sides by gilded bars with blue fillets and closed above by floral scrolling. At the bottom, two putti support the Visconti–Sforza coat of arms, flanked by two trees and the initials 'G Z'.

In the miniature which precedes the opening of the work the kneeling author is shown offering the text to a figure who was once supposed to be Galeazzo Maria. It is now thought to represent his father, Francesco. Galeazzo Maria was only sixteen years old in 1461, and cannot therefore be the standing man with grey hair, upon whose head God is placing a crown, symbolizing ducal dignity. The background of the scene is defined by a fence and a turquoise sky from which a tree and white arabesques stand out. The miniature has been attributed to the so-called 'Ippolita Master' on stylistic grounds. This artist decorated the Libretto of the privileges granted to the convent of San Sigismondo in Cremona in 1464; in the scene showing the marriage of Francesco and Bianca Maria Visconti, the representation of the Duke is very similar to the figure in this manuscript. Similarly, the arabesque motifs in the sky are also found in another manuscript by this artist, the Carthusian Missal in the Biblioteca Braidense in Milan.

Some scholars believe that the illumination in the present manuscript was executed not by the 'Ippolita Master' himself, but by his workshop, since there is a certain rigidity in the execution of the figures and the use of colour is somewhat uniform.

ON imerito udlem sere
niſſime comes ad operis
tanti quod ego q̃ q̃ indi
gnus confitiendum acce
pi laudem explicandam

PETRARCH, Canzoniere and Trionfi

Florence, Biblioteca Medicea Laurenziana

PLUT. 41. 1, FOLS. VIIIv–IX

THE MANUSCRIPT WAS COPIED IN SIENA in 1463 by Jacobus Macarius
Venetus, who signed his name on fol. 183.

The decoration includes illuminated initials and a border framing the text
on fol. 1. In the lower margin of the page, the space reserved for the coat of
arms of the patron who commissioned the work has been left blank.

The full-page portraits of Petrarch and Laura on the two pages preceding
the text are particularly noteworthy. Although they are not considered to be
contemporary with the manuscript, they were not added many years later. Their
similarity to a Venetian woodcut of 1540 has been noted; they are therefore
thought to be either the source of that engraving or to derive from a common
model.

MATTEO PALMIERI, Città di vita
(City of Life)

Florence, Biblioteca Medicea Laurenziana

PLUT. 40. 53, FOL. 41V

THE WORK IN THIS MANUSCRIPT, written by Matteo Palmieri, a Florentine writer and politician (1406–1475), deals with the qualities that a good citizen should possess. The structure of the poem is based on that of the *Divine Comedy*. It is subdivided into one hundred chapters and recounts the poet's fantastic voyage, guided by the Cumaean Sibyl, through the Elysian Fields, where he witnesses the descent of the angels among men to form souls. The wicked are condemned and the virtuous are destined for heavenly bliss. The poem, written in *terza rima*, is accompanied by the commentary of Leonardo Dati.

From the colophon on fol. 301 we learn that this copy was made in 1463 by the scribe who ends his work with the motto '*Omnium rerum vicissitudo est*' and is to be identified with Neri di Filippo Rinuccini. The decoration is attributed to the painter and illuminator Francesco Botticini. It consists of representations of the celestial Sphere, the zodiac (fol. 41v) and the symbols of the constellations, drawn in pen and painted in watercolour; there is also a fine frontispiece with white vine scroll decoration (fol. 11), with the coat of arms of the Palmieri family in the lower margin. It is likely that the manuscript was commissioned by a member of the family.

As some of the leaves have been stained by water, it is thought that the manuscript was damaged in the flood of 1557.

tellexerit ostendatur: & erunt
hæc omnia mente tenenda illis
qui ea quæ sequuntur recte in
telligere uolunt;

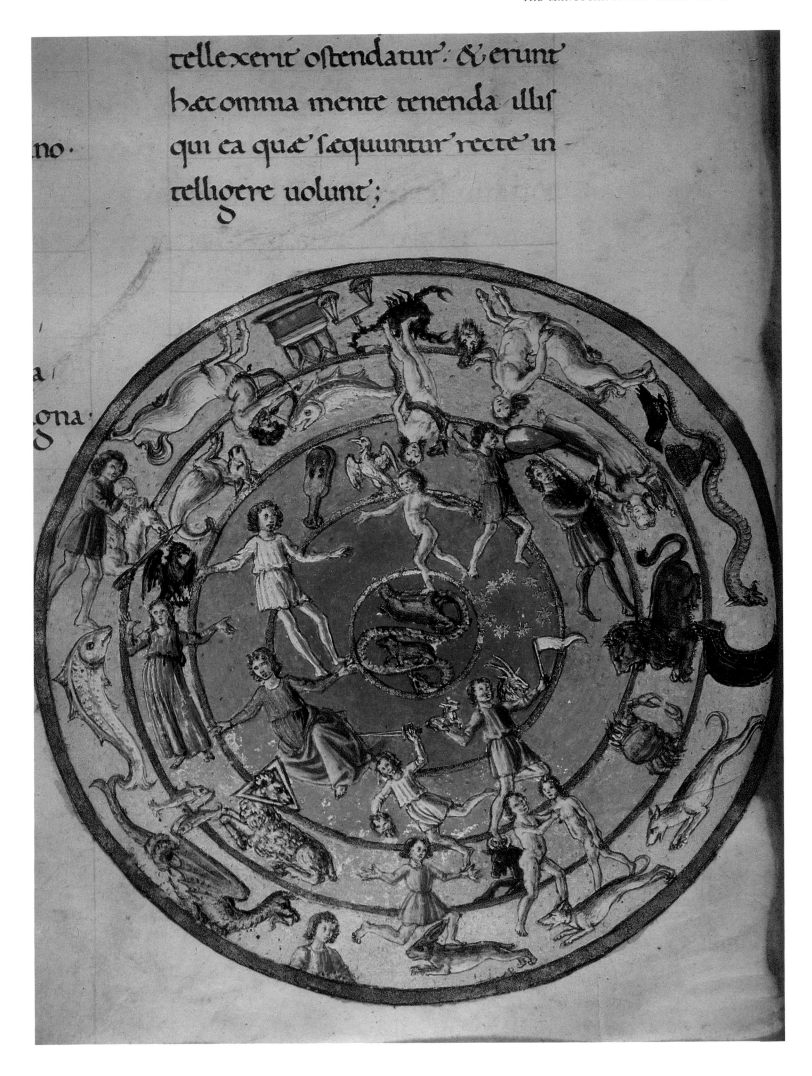

BIBLE (Bible of Borso d'Este)

Modena, Biblioteca Estense

LAT. 422-423 (= V. G. 12 AND 13), VOL. I, FOLS. 5V, 112, 110V

THIS LATIN BIBLE is known as the Bible of Borso d'Este. Numerous archival documents reveal that it was executed between 1445 and 1461 for Borso, Duke of Ferrara, who wanted to endow the ducal library with a manuscript of exceptional beauty.

The text was copied in two columns by the Milanese scribe Pietro Paolo Marone on parchment specially prepared in Bologna by the stationer (*cartolaio*) Giovanni della Badia. Some of the most famous illuminators of the time, such as Taddeo Crivelli, Franco de' Russi, Marco dell'Avogaro, Giorgio d'Alemagna and Girolamo da Cremona worked on the decoration, as well as numerous lesser artists.

The documentation concerning the years when the work was in progress, and the document detailing the final payment of 1465, provide precious information on the input of the various named artists in the decoration of the manuscript, even though careful stylistic analysis has shown that other artists who are not mentioned in the payments also contributed to the project. It should be noted that despite the diversity of styles and the collaboration of such a large number of illuminators, the artistic unity of the work was never compromised, thanks to the framework which had been stipulated. Particular attention should be paid to the Ferrarese style of border decoration, where Borso's devices and mottos appear amid the spirals and gold discs on the acanthus leaves and white vine scrolls.

Two of the pages shown here represent respectively the beginning of Genesis (fol. 5v) and the beginning of Kings (fol. 112). In the detail from fol. 110v, Ruth is shown receiving the grain to be taken to the house of Boaz.

The Bible was divided from the start into two volumes of 311 and 393 leaves: the first contains most of the Old Testament, the second the last part of the Old Testament and the New Testament. It was bound in crimson velvet by Gregorio di Gasparino between 1461 and 1462, and the binding was furnished with silver fittings attributed to Amadio da Milano.

GIOVANNI MARCANOVA,
Collectio antiquitatum

Modena, Biblioteca Estense

LAT. 992 (= α. L. 5. 15), FOL. 27

THIS MANUSCRIPT CONTAINS descriptions of a number of Roman monuments followed by eighteen imaginary scenes and a collection of inscriptions taken from monuments from all over Italy. Giovanni Marcanova, who composed and copied the main text, began the work in Padua and completed it in Bologna in 1465; he dedicated it to Domenico Malatesta Novello, the Lord of Cesena. The manuscript is of fundamental importance as one of the most significant examples of the interest of the humanists of northern Italy in antiquity and classical inscriptions.

The inscriptions were copied by the Veronese humanist and calligrapher Felice Feliciano. Some of the drawings are attributed to the Bolognese painter, Marco Zoppo. The page illustrated here shows two buildings: one circular and the other a basilica-shaped structure surmounted by a spiral column. The foreground is occupied by a fruit and chicken market; a young naked man on a high pedestal in front of the crenellated walls holds up a basin full of fruit.

The manuscript never reached Malatesta, who died in 1465, and it probably remained in Marcanova's library until it passed to the monastery of San Giovanni di Verdara in Padua on his death in 1467, together with his collection of books.

PLINY THE ELDER, Naturalis historia

Ravenna, Biblioteca Classense

INC. 670, VOL. I, FOL. 19; VOL. II, FOLS. 268, 197

IN THIS MONUMENTAL WORK, Pliny, an imperial official, historian and scholar who lived in the first century AD, has left us a kind of universal encyclopaedia in which he set out a summary of all human knowledge. The work was very popular among the humanists, and circulated not only in manuscript form but also in printed editions. This incunable was printed in Venice in 1469 by Johann of Speyer, a printer from the German Palatinate. He and his brother Wendelin introduced printing to Venice after obtaining the privilege of printing with movable type from the Venetian Republic.

The copy in the Biblioteca Classense is decorated with initials of the type known as *littera mantiniana*, named after Mantegna (as on fols. 19 and 268), which was invented in Padua in the 1450s. In this type of initial the letters are painted to appear three-dimensional. A beautiful frontispiece opens the first volume, and in the second volume there is an initial 'M', on fol. 197 inserted in a classical niche and decorated with foliate motifs and a nude female figure. In the lower margin are painted two centaurs supporting a shield for a coat of arms which has been completely erased.

The decoration, which is of exceptionally high quality, is attributed to the Paduan artist Giovanni Vendramin, who was active between 1466 and 1509. It has been suggested that the incunable was intended for the Bishop of Padua, Iacopo Zeno, for whom Vendramin and his workshop illuminated many volumes.

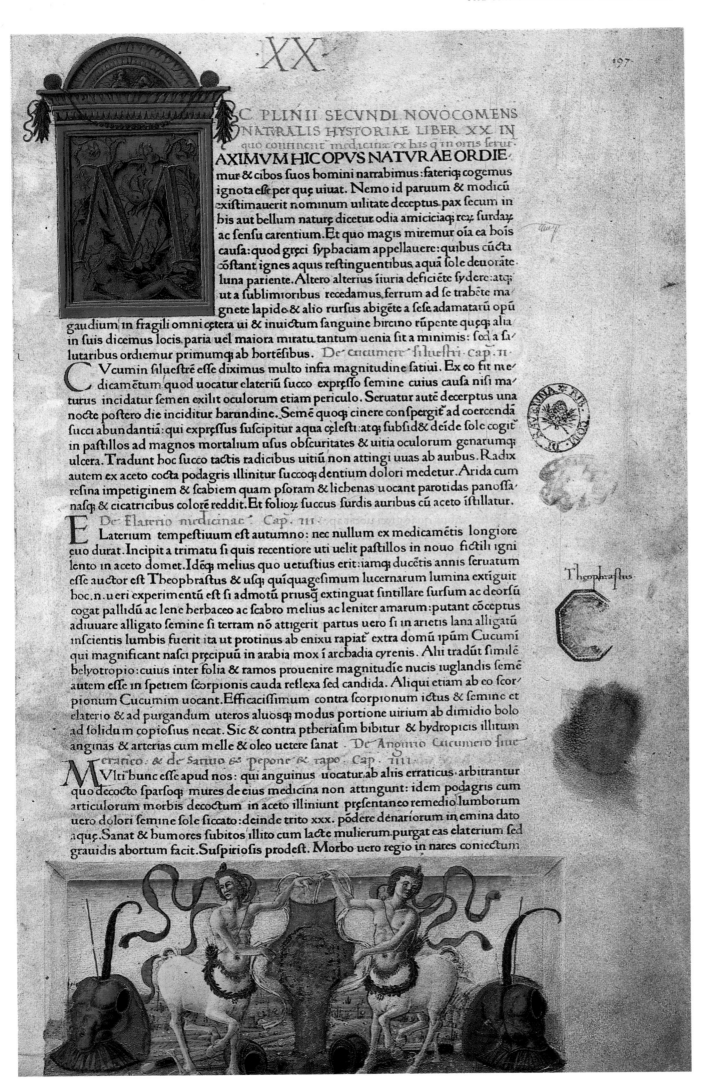

XX

C. PLINII SECVNDI NOVOCOMENS
NATVRALIS HYSTORIAE LIBER XX. IN
quo continent medicinae ex his q in ortis serut

AXIMVM HIC OPVS NATVRAE ORDIE
mur & cibos suos homini narrabimus: fateriq; cogemus
ignota esse per quę uiuat. Nemo id paruum & modicū
existimauerit nominum utilitate deceptus. pax secum in
his aut bellum naturę dicetur odia amiciciaq; reꝓ surdaꝗ
ac sensu carentium. Et quo magis miremur oīa ea hois
causa: quod greci sypbaciam appellauere: quibus cūcta
cōstant ignes aquis restinguentibus. aquā sole deuorāte.
luna pariente. Altero alterius iuria deficiēte sydere: atꝗ
ut a sublimioribus recedamus. ferrum ad se trabēte ma
gnete lapide. & alio rursus abigēte a sese adamatarū opū
gaudium in fragili omni cętera ui & inuictum sanguine bircino rūpente quęq; alia
in suis dicemus locis. paria uel maiora miratu tantum uenia sit a minimis: sed a sa
lutaribus ordiemur primumq; ab hortēsibus. De cucumere siluestri. cap. ii.

C Vcumin siluestrē esse diximus multo infra magnitudine satiui. Ex eo sit me
dicamētum quod uocatur elateriū succo expresso semine cuius causa nisi ma
turus incidatur semen exilit oculorum etiam periculo. Seruatur autē decerptus una
nocte postero die inciditur barundine. Semē quoq; cinere conspergit ad coercendā
succi abundantia: qui expressus suscipitur aqua cęlesti: atq; subsid& deide sole cogit
in pastillos ad magnos mortalium usus obscuritates & uitia oculorum genarumq;
ulcera. Tradunt hoc succo tactis radicibus uitiū non attingi uuas ab auibus. Radix
autem ex aceto cocta podagris illinitur succoq; dentium dolori medetur. Arida cum
resina impetiginem & scabiem quam psoram & lichenas uocant parotidas panossa
nasꝗ & cicatricibus colorē reddit. Et folioꝝ succus surdis auribus cū aceto istillatur.

E De Elaterio medicinae. Cap. iii.
Laterium tempestiuum est autumno: nec nullum ex medicamētis longiore
euo durat. Incipit a trimatu si quis recentiore uti uelit pastillos in nouo fictili igni
lento in aceto domet. Ideꝗ melius quo uetustius erit: iamꝗ ducētis annis seruatum
esse auctor est Theopbrastus & usꝗ quiquagesimum lucernarum lumina extiguit
boc. n. ueri experimentū est si admotū priusꝗ extinguat sintillare sursum ac deorsū
cogat pallidū ac lene berbaceo ac scabro melius ac leniter amarum: putant cōceptus
adiuuare alligato semine si terram nō attigerit partus uero si in arietis lana alligatū
inscientis lumbis fuerit ita ut protinus ab enixu rapiat̄ extra domū ipūm Cucumi
qui magnificant nasci precipuū in arabia mox ī arcbadia cyrenis. Alii tradūt similē
belyotropio: cuius inter folia & ramos prouenire magnitudie nucis iuglandis semē
autem esse in spetiem scorpionis cauda reflexa sed candida. Aliqui etiam ab eo scor
pionum Cucumim uocant. Efficacissimum contra scorpionum ictus & semine et
elaterio & ad purgandum uteros aluosq; modus portione uirium ab dimidio bolo
ad solidu m copiosius necat. Sic & contra ptheriasim bibitur & bydropicis illitum
anginas & arterias cum melle & oleo uetere sanat. De Anginio Cucumero siue
eratico. & de satiuo & pepone & rapo. Cap. iiii.

M Vltū bunc esse apud nos: qui anguinus uocatur. ab aliis erraticus. arbitrantur
quo decocto sparsoq; mures de eius medicina non attingunt: idem podagris cum
articulorum morbis decoctum in aceto illiniunt presentaneo remedio. lumborum
uero dolori semine sole siccato: deinde trito xxx. pōdere denariorum in emina dato
aquę. Sanat & bumores subitos illito cum lacte mulierum. purgat eas elaterium sed
grauidis abortum facit. Suspiriosis prodest. Morbo uero regio in nares coniectum

BOOK OF HOURS

Palermo, Biblioteca Centrale

DEP. MUSEO 6, FOL. 63

THIS SMALL MANUSCRIPT, which comes from the Benedictine monastery of San Martino alle Scale near Palermo, is a book for private devotion. It basically contains the Offices for the Virgin, for the Holy Cross and for the Dead, preceded by the calendar, but many leaves are missing. The initials to the text, in gold on coloured grounds, are flanked by historiated scenes set within arched frames with three lines of text in the space below.

The miniature reproduced here shows Bathsheba standing near a fountain dressed in transparent muslin; David, wearing a turban and crown, looks on from the window of a palace in the background. The detailed background is painted in tones of green, grey and blue. The border is wider along the bottom and outer margins of the page than in the inner margin. It is painted on a liquid gold ground and decorated with acanthus leaves interspersed with other realistically painted foliate motifs, as well as flowers, butterflies and the coat of arms of the noble Campo family of Palermo; these arms are also found on many other pages of the manuscript. The illumination has been attributed on stylistic grounds to the Ghent and Bruges school of Alexander Bening, who was active between 1469 and 1519. His art is characterized by the animation and plasticity of the scenes, executed with firm strokes and a pleasing expressive freedom. These give the miniatures, painted in soft colours, a delightful impressionistic quality.

PETRARCH, Canzoniere and Trionfi

Venice, Biblioteca Marciana

INC. VEN. 546, FOL. 9

THIS IS A COPY of the *editio princeps* of Petrarch's *Canzoniere*, which was the first book in Italian to be printed in Venice. It was printed in 1470 by Wendelin of Speyer, the brother of Johann of Speyer who introduced printing to Venice with his edition of the works of Cicero, printed there in 1469. The brothers came from Speyer in Germany and opened the first printing-house in Venice in 1468 after Johann had obtained a privilege for printing with movable type from the Venetian Signoria.

Already with his first edition Johann demonstrated that an efficient organization for the sale of books was in place in Venice, for the three hundred copies that he printed of his Cicero sold immediately, as indeed did the further three hundred of the second edition. In 1470 Johann died and Wendelin took over the business. He plunged at once into intense activity. Already in 1470 he managed to print fifteen books, and he printed a further ten in each of the following years. The Biblioteca Marciana possesses not only this present copy of the edition of Petrarch's Italian works, which is printed on paper, but also another copy, printed on parchment. This edition of Petrarch had such a success that by 1516 no further copies of it were obtainable.

The text opens with an index of the poems; the names of the author and printer, and the date of printing, appear only in the printer's colophon at the end. The opening pages of both the *Canzoniere* on fol. 9 and the *Trionfi* on fol. 145 are decorated with rich and ample borders of spiralling penwork decorated with leaves, flowers, fruit and animals. In the lower border of fol. 9 Petrarch and Laura appear seated beside a tree on a branch of which hangs the coat of arms of the Priuli family of Venice. The style of the decoration has been compared to the work of Girolamo da Cremona (1435–1483), one of the illuminators who collaborated on the decoration of the Bible of Borso d'Este (for which see p. 186) and on a Missal for the Gonzaga family. The activity of Girolamo is documented at Padua, Siena and Florence, but his finest work is to be found in the decoration of several incunables printed in Venice, including the *Decretum* of Gratian of 1474 and the Aristotle of 1483.

OI CHASCOLTATE INRI
me sparse ilsuono
Diquei sospiri ondio nudriual core
Insulmio primo giouenile errore
quandera in parte altro huom da quel chi sono
del uario stile inchio piango & ragiono
fra le uane speranze el uan dolore
oue sia chi per proua intenda amore
spero trouar pieta non che perdono
Ma ben ueggio hor si comealpopol tutto
fauola fui gran tempo onde souente
dime medesmo meco miuergogno
& delmio uaneggiar uergogna el fructo
el pentersi el conoscer chiaramente
che quanto piace almondo e breue sogno

ERA il giorno chal sol si scoloraro
per la pieta del suo factore irai
quando ifui preso & non mene guardai
che ibe uostri occhi donna mi legaro
tempo non mi parea da far riparo
contra colpi damor pero mandai
secur senza sospecto onde i miei guai
nel commune dolor sincominciaro
Trouommi amor del tutto disarmato
& aperta lauia per gliocchi alcore
che di lagrime son facti uscio & uarco
pero al mio parer non li fu honore
ferir me de saetta inquello stato
a uoi armata non monstrar pur larco

VIRGIL, Works

Vatican City, Biblioteca Apostolica Vaticana

URB. LAT. 350, FOL. 45V (DETAIL AND COMPLETE PAGE)

THIS MANUSCRIPT, which contains the *Eclogues*, *Georgics* and *Aeneid*, followed by pseudo-Virgilian works, is carefully decorated with white vine scrolling, used both for the initials and the borders, enriched with fruit, and inhabited by birds and deer.

The only full-page miniature, on fol. 45v, is set within a large architectural frame, on the pediment of which is written verse 289 of the second book of the *Aeneid*: 'HEU FUGE NATE DEA TEQUE. HIS AIT ERIPE FLAMMIS'. Aeneas is shown carrying his father Anchises on his shoulders and leading his son Ascanius by the hand, as they make their way towards the boats, leaving Troy in flames. Above the portico framing the scene, two winged putti support the Garter of England set with pearls and precious stones and with the motto '*hony soyt qui mal y pense*', within which an eagle supports the coat of arms of Federico da Montefeltro, Duke of Urbino; his emblems are also found on fol. 2v and fol. 46v.

The manuscript was written by an anonymous Florentine scribe, to whom four further manuscripts have been attributed. He may be identifiable with Mariotto Nori who worked for Guarino at Ferrara in the 1420s.

The original white vine decoration also suggests a Florentine origin and a date around 1440, while the large miniature shown and the title to the *Aeneid* on the facing page were added by Guglielmo Giraldi in about 1480, presumably at the time that the codex was acquired by Federico da Montefeltro.

BOOK OF HOURS

Florence, Biblioteca Nazionale Centrale

BANCO RARI 332, FOL. 171V

T HIS MANUSCRIPT has lost a number of leaves at the beginning which would have had miniatures; the remaining leaves are decorated with borders of foliage strewn with flowers and fruit and by eight large full-page miniatures set in arched frames and surrounded by borders decorated with flowers as well as animals and human figures. The miniatures are of the Nativity, the Annunciation to the Shepherds, the Flight into Egypt, Pentecost, the communion of a dying man and his funeral, and the stories of Susanna and Saint Mary Magdalen.

Both the script of the manuscript and its decoration suggest that this book of Hours was produced in the 1470s in the workshop of a not particularly refined French artist who is rather repetitive in his treatment of borders but is more skilled in the accurate representation of landscapes and buildings. The figures with their long faces, the design of the clothes and the typology of the animals represented in the manuscript are all close to the style of an artist active at Paris around 1470, the 'Master of Adelaide of Savoy', that is to be seen in the book of Hours at Chantilly after which he is named and in a fragment from another book of Hours now in the collection of Everett and Ann McNear of Chicago.

On fol. 171v, reproduced here, we see several episodes from the story of Susanna, which is found in a deuterocanonical appendix to the Old Testament Book of Daniel. According to this account Susanna was surprised at her bath by two Jewish elders who were judges; they were attracted by her and tried to seduce her. She repulsed their advances and in revenge they accused her of flagrant adultery and condemned her to death. She was saved by the intervention of the prophet Daniel, who unmasked the two elders; they were then stoned to death.

MISSAL

Milan, Biblioteca Trivulziana

2165, FOL. 9

THIS OPULENT MANUSCRIPT, one of the most beautiful codices of the Ferrarese school, has decoration on almost all its 426 leaves. This decoration comprises one full-page miniature, five miniatures surrounded by borders with scenes including figures, 237 with borders containing medallions with figures, 113 historiated initials and 136 initials with foliate motifs.

The manuscript was made for Ercole I d'Este, elected Duke of Ferrara in 1471, whose coat of arms and emblems appear on fol. 9 and in some medallions. The decoration was executed by two artists in close collaboration. One has been identified as Martino da Modena, a very fine illuminator who was active in the Po area from the 1470s. He is considered to have executed the page shown here, with the beginning of the Mass for the first Sunday in Advent. It is decorated with a wide border of stylized flowers set on a ground of gold filigree divided into compartments. In the circular medallions are shown the archangel Gabriel, God the Father, the Virgin, a putto seated in the Este diamond ring and a warrior in profile. In the lower border is an enchanting scene with numerous putti, some playing musical instruments; those at the centre support the Este coat of arms beneath a sumptuous awning; in the background there is a rocky landscape with strange human-shaped clouds in the sky. Further Este emblems are set in the top border. The historiated initial 'A' of the text shows David in penitence.

In this manuscript, Martino's style is still close to that of his father, Giorgio d'Alemagna, who was Borso d'Este's favourite illuminator. Some critics consider that Giorgio was the other main illuminator who worked on the decoration of this Missal, together with other minor artists.

GUILLAUME FICHET, Rhetorica

Venice, Biblioteca Marciana

MEMBRANACEI 53, FOL. 1

ONE OF CARDINAL BESSARION'S most influential cultural contributions was his exposition of Platonic philosophy, which he undertook not only to explain the Greek philosopher's thought and to demonstrate that it did not contradict Christian thought, but also to refute the assertions of George Trapezuntius, who considered Plato to be a symbol of moral depravation. The cardinal's thought is expounded in his work, *In calumniatorem Platonis*, written in 1459 and issued in a printed edition of three hundred copies ten years later in 1469 with the title *Adversus calumniatorem Platonis*. Bessarion's work enjoyed success not only on account of his clear exposition of the philosophical concepts that it treated, but also because printing ensured that it had a rapid diffusion.

Bessarion also made use of the new technique of printing, which assisted this rapid circulation of texts, for the edition of his *Orationes* in 1471. The work was entrusted to Guillaume Fichet, a prior, teacher of rhetoric and rector at the Sorbonne, who, in association with Jean Heynlin, had brought three German printers to Paris in 1470 and set up the first printing press in France. One of the first books that Fichet published was his own *Rhetorica*, which was also printed in 1471. The copy at the Biblioteca Marciana is printed on parchment and was given to Bessarion by Fichet, who was in this case both the author and printer.

The miniature reproduced here, which precedes the text, shows the cardinal seated on the left receiving the work from the author. The scene is framed by spiralling tendrils, floral motifs and birds; in the lower margin, the space reserved for Bessarion's coat of arms, surmounted by a cardinal's hat, has been left blank. A further portrait of Cardinal Bessarion is included in another copy of the same work, now in London. In this copy the miniature shows Fichet offering the work to Pope Sixtus IV, with Bessarion by his side.

CRISTOFORO LANDINO,
Disputationes camaldulenses

Vatican City, Biblioteca Apostolica Vaticana

URB. LAT. 508, FLYLEAF

THE MANUSCRIPT CONTAINS the *Disputationes* by Landino (1424–1492), who was an important exponent of Florentine Neoplatonism. The work was composed between April and December 1472 and consists of a series of conversations held at Camaldoli between the author, Lorenzo de' Medici 'il Magnifico', Leon Battista Alberti and Marsilio Ficino, concerning the active and contemplative life.

The transcription of the Vatican codex is attributed to the Florentine scribe Gabriele da Pistoia and it was illuminated by Francesco d'Antonio del Chierico. It is the dedication copy for Federico da Montefeltro (1421–1482) and the version of his coat of arms and the devices included in the decoration suggest that it was given to him before he became Duke of Urbino in 1474.

The leaf illustrated here is glued to the inside binding of the manuscript and partly for this reason is not thought to have formed part of it originally. It has been suggested that the miniature might have been taken from a choir book, but this hypothesis would seem to be contradicted by its small dimensions. On the left it shows Federico da Montefeltro holding a book. He is recognizable by the strange shape of his nose, which he injured in a tournament in 1450. The figure on the right is thought by some scholars to be a self-portrait of the illuminator and sculptor Francesco di Giorgio Martini, to whom they attribute the miniature, but others consider it to be a portrait of Cristoforo Landino. The figure's clothing, which suggests an academic rather than an artist or a cleric, appears to contradict both hypotheses. The two figures appear to be framed in an open window, which has a Turkish carpet on the sill. Although recent scholars still believe the painting was added after the manuscript was completed, on stylistic grounds they consider the work to be by the decorator of the main manuscript, Francesco d'Antonio del Chierico, one of the finest Florentine illuminators of the second half of the fifteenth century (see p. 206).

BIBLE (Urbino Bible)

Vatican City, Biblioteca Apostolica Vaticana

VAT. LAT. 1, FOL. 27 (WHOLE PAGE AND DETAIL)

THE TWO VOLUMES which make up the Urbino Bible (MSS. Vat. lat. 1 and 2) are exceptionally large in size (596 x 442 mm). They were copied by the French scribe Hugo de Comminellis of Mézières under the direction of the bookseller and stationer (*cartolaio*) Vespasiano da Bisticci, who between about 1467 and 1480 worked on the production of many manuscripts for the library of Federico da Montefeltro. The copying of the first volume of the Bible, containing part of the Old Testament in Saint Jerome's translation, was completed on 25 February 1477; the second volume, with the rest of the Old Testament and the New Testament, was finished on 12 June 1478.

The general direction (as well as much of the execution) of the decorative scheme was entrusted to Francesco d'Antonio del Chierico. The pictorial programme, in the planning of which Vespasiano must also have participated, diverged from the subjects usually treated in Italian Bibles both of the fifteenth century and of preceding centuries. Alongside the work of Francesco there are important contributions from Domenico Ghirlandaio and his workshop, Attavante degli Attavanti, Francesco Rosselli and the 'Master of the Hamilton Xenophon'. The pages are framed with rich floral borders, decorated with candlesticks, putti, animals and birds, and with historiated medallions containing subjects closely linked to the large-scale scenes in the upper parts of the same pages which also incorporate the incipits to the text.

The large scene at the beginning of the Book of Exodus on fol. 27, the first horizontal miniature executed by Francesco in the Bible, shows the entrance of the Israelites into Egypt. The procession, which winds over a wide landscape, is made up of groups of figures characterized with great liveliness. It is possible to identify Jacob with his wife, Ruben, Simeon, Levi and Judah, Issacar, Zebulun and Benjamin, Dan and Naphtali, Gad and Asher. The six medallions set in the border contain stories from the life of Moses: Pharaoh oppressing the Israelites, the Israelites building a town, Pharaoh ordering the killing of male children, the baby Moses abandoned by the water, Moses being saved from the water and Moses being adopted.

FRANCESCO ALVAROTTI,
Consilia et allegationes

Ravenna, Biblioteca Classense

450, FOL. 2

THIS COLLECTION OF juridical texts by the canon Francesco Alvarotti (1390–1460) was copied between 1477 and 1478 by Jacopo de' Ruberiis, a cleric who was active in Rome and Dalmatia.

The frontispiece on fol. 2 includes a portrait of Alvarotti expounding a law book in the company of a seated youth, taking notes, who is too young to be identified as De' Ruberiis. The decoration of the manuscript is attributed to Girolamo da Cremona (see pp. 186, 194), although the illumination has been reworked: three strips of paper have been added to the verso, and the faces of the two figures have been heavily retouched. The medallions in the border are of finer execution. They show Roman emperors set in frames simulating classical-style bas reliefs in porphyry.

DANTE ALIGHIERI, Divine Comedy

Vatican City, Biblioteca Apostolica Vaticana

URB. LAT. 365, FOLS. 177, 25

THIS COPY OF THE *Divine Comedy* was executed for Federico da Montefeltro, whose coat of arms is painted on folios 1 and 97. The codex was written by Matteo de' Contugi of Volterra, a scribe who worked in Mantua for the Gonzaga family, for Federico da Montefeltro in Ferrara and later in Urbino, and after Federico's death, for Ercole I d'Este in Ferrara.

From one of Contugi's letters dated 1478 we learn that the manuscript had already been copied by that time and was in Ferrara waiting to be decorated. The first part was illuminated by Guglielmo Giraldi from Ferrara. He used limpid and bright colours to achieve the surreal backgrounds in the illustrations for the cantos of Hell, which are characterized by rocky landscapes set against brilliant blue skies and are peopled by highly dramatic figures. Giraldi's decoration ends at fol. 72 and is followed by that of an artist very close in style who has been identified as his nephew Alessandro Leoni. A third artist who follows in turn is thought to be Franco de' Russi, also from Ferrara, who worked on the Bible of Borso d'Este and was active in the Veneto and at the court of Urbino. It is also possible to distinguish the work of a fourth contemporary illuminator, whose style is influenced by the work of Giraldi.

As we have seen, documentary evidence shows that the manuscript was in Ferrara in 1478; the decoration on which Giraldi had started work for the Urbino library in 1480 was interrupted by the death of Federico in 1482. From fol. 171 on, the miniatures were completed by an anonymous sixteenth-century artist. The first page illustrated here is for Canto XXVIII of Purgatory and shows Dante with Statius, Virgil and Matilda on the banks of the river Lethe; in the other page, illustrating Canto X of Hell, we see Dante and Farinata before a sarcophagus in which are Cavalcanti and a further unidentified figure.

GOSPELS

Vatican City, Biblioteca Apostolica Vaticana

URB. LAT. 10, FOL. 175 (DETAIL AND WHOLE PAGE)

THIS MANUSCRIPT, and those of the Bible and the *Divine Comedy*, are among the most beautiful codices produced for Federico da Montefeltro, the Duke of Urbino. It was copied in an elegant hand by Matteo de' Contugi of Volterra (see p. 210), one of the scribes who worked for the ducal library and to whom seven Urbino manuscripts are attributed, all of which are datable to after August 1474, when Federico took on the title of Duke of Urbino and papal *gonfaloniere* (standard bearer); the coats of arms which they bear are accompanied by the letters 'F D': *Federicus Dux*.

The decoration consists of borders of white interlace with finely decorated medallions and full-page miniatures set in architectural frames.

Fol. 175 shows Saint John seated writing on the side of a rugged mountain with a castle at the summit; on the sea in the background to the right there are ships and there are buildings in the distance on the left. In the sky are the seven candelabra which appeared to the prophet of Patmos. The scene is set in an ornate frame with candlesticks in the left and right margins; these are united by festoons in the upper margin, on either side of which is written 'FE DUX', identifying the owner of the manuscript. The initial and incipit to the text, written in capitals, are set in the base of the monumental frame. Below an eagle supports the primitive version of the Montefeltro arms.

The magnificent miniature, executed between 1480 and 1482, is an elegant example of the Ferrarese school; it was begun by Guglielmo Giraldi and completed by Franco de' Russi.

SANDRO BOTTICELLI,
Illustrations for
the Divine Comedy

Vatican City, Biblioteca Apostolica Vaticana

REG. LAT. 1896 A, FOL. 99

Botticelli's cycle of illustrations for the *Divine Comedy* are on ninety-two folios, eighty-five of which are in Berlin and the remaining seven in the Vatican Library. The Vatican leaves, which once belonged to Queen Christina of Sweden, were bought in 1690 by Pope Alexander VIII.

The drawings were executed in silver point: in many cases they have been reworked in pen, and in some cases coloured with tempera. Their existence is documented by Vasari and other early sources; it is likely that they were begun after 1482, when Botticelli returned from Rome, where he had been working on the Sistine Chapel. The drawings were never finished, either as a result of the Medici's expulsion from Florence or of the death of Lorenzo di Pierfrancesco de' Medici, the cousin of Lorenzo 'il Magnifico', who is thought to have commissioned them.

Botticelli is thought to have worked also on another series of drawings, which show similarities to these, illustrating Landino's commentary to the *Divine Comedy*.

The partly coloured page shown here illustrates Canto X of Hell.

BOOK OF HOURS (La Flora)

Naples, Biblioteca Vittorio Emanuele III

I. B. 51, FOLS. 9, 135V

THIS CODEX, known as *La Flora*, is one of the most precious manuscripts in the library in Naples and one of the most notable examples of Franco-Flemish illumination of the Ghent and Bruges school. The work follows the usual scheme, with the calendar at the beginning, each month being laid out over two pages, illustrated not only with the signs of the zodiac, but also with allegorical scenes within wide architectural frames; fol. 9 illustrates the month of July. The text is decorated with over one hundred miniatures (thirty-six are full-page and sixty-six are smaller in size), many of which are framed by wide borders decorated with flowers and fruit interspersed with insects and butterflies. A great range of colours is used in the decoration, and it is abundantly enriched in gold.

Recent studies have shown that the decoration of the manuscript is the fruit of collaboration between a number of illuminators working under the direction of an entrepreneur who succeeded in imposing unity and balance on the whole.

Twenty-eight of the thirty-six full-page miniatures were executed by Simon Marmion, whose art is characterized by a marked naturalism. Marmion did superb work for King Philip the Good, which earned him the name of 'Prince of Illumination'. Gerard Horenbout, the Flemish painter of the Vienna *Hortulus animae*, who also worked at the Hungarian court between the end of the fifteenth century and the first two decades of the sixteenth, had a role of primary importance in the production of this manuscript. Together with the 'Master of the Dresden Hours' he executed the floral decoration, while the style of the landscapes suggests the influence, if not the direct collaboration, of Alexander Bening.

On fol. 135v the Flight into Egypt is shown set within a rich architectural frame. The inclusion of Charles VIII's coat of arms in the decoration on fol. 2v has led critics to suppose that the codex was made for the French king, but the most recent theory is that the arms were added later and that the manuscript came into the king's possession after it had been completed. The evidence of the calendar would date it between 1483 and 1498.

CAESAR, Commentaries translated into French by Robert Gaguin

Florence, Biblioteca Medicea Laurenziana

PLUT. 62. 8, FOL. 105

T HIS MANUSCRIPT CONTAINS the French version of Caesar's work by Robert Gaguin, a French theologian and humanist (1433–1501), who was General of the Trinitarian order. He taught at the Sorbonne and was entrusted with various diplomatic missions to Italy.

The colophon at the end of the manuscript tells us that it was written in 1485 and is the dedication copy presented to Charles VIII of France. It also informs us of the translator's name. At least two miniatures were removed from the manuscript long ago. On fol. 105, in the surviving miniature reproduced here, Vercingetorix, King of the Averni, who supported the rebellion of the Gallic tribes against the Romans and gained command, is shown with his soldiers in the foreground. The background landscape is typically French; the wide countryside, dotted with towns and castles, is traversed by the River Loire. The marginal border is decorated with floral motifs and animals, and also includes the coat of arms of the King of France, repeated several times.

PAUSANIAS, Description of Greece

Florence, Biblioteca Medicea Laurenziana

PLUT. 56. 11, FOL. 1

THIS GREEK CODEX WAS WRITTEN by the Cretan John Rhosus, who was the favourite scribe of Lorenzo de' Medici 'il Magnifico' and of Cardinal Bessarion. His signed colophon on fol. 282 states that the work was completed in Rome on 10 September 1485.

All later surviving manuscripts containing the work of Pausanias are supposed to derive from an ancient codex which had belonged to the Florentine humanist Niccolò Niccoli before it passed to the library of the Convent of San Marco in Florence. This manuscript, however, seems to be an exception and may derive from a different exemplar belonging to Lorenzo di Pierfrancesco de' Medici, that Giovanni Lorenzi, the librarian of Pope Innocent VIII, asked to borrow in the spring of 1485 and managed to obtain with the help of Angelo Poliziano.

The decoration consists of an elegant ornamental border of candelabra interspersed with foliate motifs, and embellished with fruit, flowers, birds and butterflies, arranged in a composite, asymmetric yet harmonious whole. Pausanias appears within the initial, holding a copy of his work; the coat of arms which was once in the centre of the lower border has been entirely erased and it is not now possible to tell for whom this exquisite manuscript was made.

The illumination, which shows how the artist originally attempted to conform to Greek cultural conventions, has been attributed to one of the busiest artists of the second half of the fifteenth century, active in Rome from about 1463 and known as 'Pseudo-Michele da Carrara'.

It has been noted how in the fifteenth century copies of the work of Pausanias were still being copied in Greek from Greek manuscripts, and that despite the interest displayed by humanists in the archaeology and geography of ancient Greece, no one thought to make a Latin version of his text. The first Latin translation (it is incomplete and known only from MS. CCVII, Biblioteca Capitolare, Verona) was initiated by the humanist Domizio Calderini, using a copy of a Greek manuscript that he commissioned himself in 1477. It was printed in Vienna in 1500.

CAESAR, Commentaries

Rome, Biblioteca Casanatense

453, FOLS. 1V–1, 199

THIS BEAUTIFUL MANUSCRIPT, datable to the late fifteenth century, is very refined both in its writing and its decoration. It was copied in Rome by the famous Paduan scribe Bartolomeo Sanvito (1435–1512/1513). He also wrote the beautiful coloured epigraphic capitals in alternating lines of gold, blue, red, green, and purple, which were his speciality and which are used here for headings and incipits (see fols. 1, 199 illustrated).

Fol. 1 is framed by a classical niche with putti, shields and arms. In the lower margin there is a battle scene in monochrome gold on a blue ground. In the initial 'G' Caesar is shown talking to his soldiers against a background of ancient Roman buildings. The leaf stained pink preceding fol. 1, which may not originally have belonged to this manuscript, has on its verso, facing fol. 1, a miniature of a triumphal procession passing through an arch which is probably by the same artist. It is executed in an antiquarian style in red and silver chiaroscuro on the pink tinted ground. A further fourteen initials with classical motifs (a fine example can be seen on fol. 199), decorate the beginning of each book. Various hypotheses have been advanced as to the identity of the illuminator; the Paduan/Roman school of illumination and Bartolomeo Sanvito of Padua (the scribe of the manuscript) have both been suggested. Recent criticism attributes the decoration to a Paduan artist working in Rome, perhaps identifiable as Gaspare da Padova.

· XIV ·

terrā prouec̄tus, duode trigesimo die: Ideo q̄d tempestatibus ī
portubus cohibebatur, ad vrbem Romam uenit;

C·IVLII·CAES·COMMĒ
TARIORVM BELLI HI
SPANI·OPII AVT HIR
TII LIBER·XIV·

HARNA
CE SVPE
RATO·AFRI
CA RECE
PTA·QVI

EX IIS PRAELIIS CVM

adolescente. CN. Pompeio profugissent: cū & ulterioris Hispa
niæ potitus ēēt: dum Cæsar muneribus dandis in Italia deti
netur, quo facilius præsidia comparar&: Pompeius in fide uni
usaiusq; ciuitatis confugere coepit· Ita ptim precibus: ptim ui
bene magna comparata manu prouinciam uastare coepit· Qui
bus in rebus ciuitates nonullæ sua sponte auxilia mittebant.
Item nonullæ contra portas claudebant· Ex qbus siqud oppida

MARTIANUS CAPELLA, De nuptiis Mercurii et Philologiae

Venice, Biblioteca Marciana

LAT. XIV. 35 (= 4054), FOLS. 134V, 149V

THIS WORK DEALS IN DEPTH with the seven Liberal Arts – grammar, dialectic, rhetoric, arithmetic, geometry, astronomy and music – within the framework of the romantic story of the marriage of Mercury and Philosophy but has a profoundly didactic content. It was composed between 330 and 429 AD and was very popular in the Middle Ages, becoming the basis of culture and teaching, since it contained exhaustive definitions of the individual disciplines.

The names of both the scribe and illuminator of this fine Florentine copy of Martianus Capella are found in the manuscript. The signature of the scribe, Alessandro da Verrazzano, is on fol. 204. Born in 1453, he was an independent scribe, perhaps even a dilettante; some of his works were certainly executed as gifts for friends. The manuscripts that he signed are dated between 1477 and 1506 and many of his works were produced for illustrious patrons, such as Giovanni Cardinal of Aragon, Lorenzo di Pierfrancesco de' Medici, King Matthias Corvinus of Hungary, the King of Portugal, and Ippolita Sforza Duchess of Calabria. The illumination is by Attavante, an important figure in Florentine illumination of the late fifteenth century. In this manuscript, which was made for the library of the King of Hungary, he signed the miniature on fol. 1: 'Attavantes Florent. pinxit'. The decoration consists of twenty-four miniatures, representing the Meetings of the Gods and the Arts of the Trivium and Quadrivium, as well as borders with floral motifs and decorated initials. The Arts are all depicted as enthroned female figures in the act of demonstrating or teaching the science they personify. Fol. 134v represents Astronomy and fol. 149v shows Music.

The manuscript, which is datable between 1485 and 1490, was bought at the end of the fifteenth century by Gioacchino Torriano, a scholar and monk at the Dominican convent of SS. Giovanni e Paolo in Venice.

HOMER, Works

Naples, Biblioteca Vittorio Emanuele III

S. Q. XIII. K. 22, FOL. IIv

THIS GREEK INCUNABLE of Homer's works was printed in Florence in 1488. It was edited by Demetrius Chalcondyles, who wrote the preface, and was printed at the expense of Bernardo de' Nerli, with contributions from his brother, Neri de' Nerli, and Donato Acciaiuoli.

The work is dedicated to Piero de' Medici, son of Lorenzo 'il Magnifico' in a letter at the beginning of the volume.

The copy in Naples is an exquisite one printed on parchment, and is thought to have been the presentation copy given to Piero de' Medici, for his full-page portrait in tempera appears on the second page preceding the text. The large-scale painting (330 x 225 mm) has been attributed to Gherardo di Giovanni, who decorated the rest of the volume with borders and illuminated initials. Another portrait of Piero is found in a medallion set in the border decorating the beginning of the *Odyssey* on fol. 224.

Not only the Medici arms, but also those of the Farnese family appear in the volume. It is thought that the Farnese arms were added later when the incunable was acquired by Alessandro Farnese, the future Pope Paul III.

PSALTER AND NEW TESTAMENT

Florence, Biblioteca Medicea Laurenziana

PLUT. 15. 17, FOL. 3, DETAIL

THIS MANUSCRIPT is the third part of a large Bible in three volumes which was made for Matthias Corvinus, King of Hungary, but left incomplete after Corvinus died in 1490. This volume contains the Psalter and the New Testament. It was the only volume to be completed; the first was only partially decorated and the second has no illumination at all.

The text of this exceptionally large manuscript, measuring 535 x 370 mm, was copied in two columns by Sigismondo de' Sigismondi, one of the most active scribes in Florence in the late fifteenth century, probably between 1489 and 1490. The two sumptuous leaves at the beginning, illuminated in Florence by Gherardo and Monte di Giovanni, are considered to be their masterpieces.

Fol. 3, with the beginning of the Psalter, written in gold on a purple ground, is richly illuminated. Around the page a wide border, enlivened with putti, lions and devices, contains numerous medallions showing biblical figures. The upper half of the text space is occupied by a large miniature representing the battle of the Israelites, led by David, against the Philistines, in front of the town of Hebron. The town is based on Florence and it is possible to make out the Loggia dei Lanzi and the Palazzo Vecchio.

Recent scholars believe that the battle scene is an allusion to the struggle against the Turks and point out that the representation of David can be taken to signify a celebration of Matthias Corvinus. When the King suddenly died, the manuscript was still in Florence. It was acquired for the Medici Library together with other as yet unfinished manuscripts that had been commissioned by Corvinus.

BOOK OF HOURS

Milan, Biblioteca Trivulziana

475, FOL. 70

THIS TINY MANUSCRIPT (112 x 85 mm) was made in the last decade of the fifteenth century for Niccolò Casati, brother-in-law to the ducal chancellor Tristano Calci, who died in 1523. It has Casati's arms on fol. 1 with the initials 'NI CA'.

The scribe was Giovan Battista de' Lorenzi, who also copied out two other famous codices in the Biblioteca Trivulziana: the *Grammar* of Donatus and the *Liber Iesus*, both made for the young Massimiliano Sforza (see pp. 238, 240). The decoration in the present manuscript consists of frames with candlesticks and jewels, five scenes with figures, showing the Presentation in the Temple (fol. 1), David in prayer and God the Father (fol. 70), the Pietà (fol. 105v), a portrait of Niccolò Casati (fol. 106) and a decorated initial (fol. 144).

The ornamentation of the page illustrated here greatly enlarged is particularly original. God the Father is depicted above a plaque bearing the heading to the Seven Penitential Psalms, with the figure of David praying below. On either side are double pilasters decorated in gold, painted to give the illusion that they, and David, are behind a torn and curling leaf on which the first lines of the text are written. In the lower margin is a bearded head with an angel holding a cornucopia on either side; the space around them is studded with pearls and varicoloured jewels.

The decoration is by an artist whose style is of Venetian derivation but who was active in Milan and worked on other Milanese manuscripts at the end of the fifteenth century. He has been called the 'Master of the Landriani Hours', after a book of Hours made for Antonio Landriani, treasurer of Ludovico il Moro, on which he worked (MS. 63 in Keble College, Oxford).

BOOK OF HOURS

Milan, Biblioteca Trivulziana

INC. E. 25, FOL. 75V

THIS EDITION of the Hours of the Virgin was printed on parchment in Venice in 1491 by Johann of Speyer and published by Lucantonio Giunta, a Florentine who was exiled as an opponent of the Medici family and took refuge in Venice, where he worked from 1489 to 1538.

The present copy, the only one known to exist in Italy, has six woodcut illustrations painted in watercolour, thirteen historiated initials with the letter 'D', and a coat of arms painted on fol. 17, which has been identified as that of the Sassolo family of Venice.

The six woodcuts illustrate the Annunciation, the Immaculate Conception, the prophet David (shown here), the Office of the Dead, the Crucifixion and Pentecost. The illustrations which are inspired by popular tradition, have somewhat rigid human figures with static expressions, and the architectural settings are reduced to a few essentials.

The woodcuts used are of the 'Malermi' type, a type which was widely used in Venice between 1490 and 1495. The name derives from the illustrations in the vernacular edition of the Bible with a commentary by Nicolò Malermi, which was printed in Venice in 1490 by Giovanni Ragazzo and Lucantonio Giunta. The woodblocks used for the woodcuts in this edition were re-used for religious books by other Venetian printers between 1493 and 1497.

ROMAN MISSAL

Florence, Biblioteca Medicea Laurenziana

EDILI 9, FOL. 8

THIS MAGNIFICENT MISSAL was copied for Florence Cathedral in 1493 by the scribe Zanobi de' Moschini, who signed his name on fol. 318v. It is decorated with very fine miniatures attributed to several different Florentine illuminators.

The detail shown here is from fol. 8, which is ornately framed by a wide border with medallions inserted in it showing God blessing the scene below, the prophets and Saint Zenobius. The upper half of the page is occupied by a large rectangular miniature of the Annunciation. On the right, the Virgin is seated praying; the Archangel Gabriel kneels on the left of the scene holding a lily, symbolizing purity. The dove of the Holy Spirit hovers above them.

The scene is set beneath a loggia; a wide landscape, in which the dome of the cathedral and, on the right, a portico similar to that of the Ospedale degli Innocenti in Florence, can be glimpsed through the open doors and windows. The painting, which is of the finest quality, is attributed to Gherardo and Monte di Giovanni, who executed most of the illumination in the manuscript.

BOOK OF HOURS

Ravenna, Biblioteca Classense

INC. 79, FOLS. 31V-32

THIS IS A COPY of a rare edition of the book of Hours printed in Paris in 1494 by Philippe Pigouchet, who signs himself '*Libraire de l'université de Paris*'. Pigouchet was active between 1484 and 1516; from 1490 to 1500 he specialized in producing books of Hours; he printed seventy-five editions in this period, and also worked for the main Parisian publishers of his time.

The decoration consists of twenty full-page engravings (that on fol. 32, shown here, represents the Annunciation to the Shepherds) and of borders with little historiated scenes and zoomorphic and foliate motifs surrounding every page. The initials to the text are coloured in gold on predominantly red or blue grounds. The engravings employed for this edition are a refined example of printed book decoration. They continued to be re-used by Pigouchet until 1496.

The incunable of the Biblioteca Classense belonged in the eighteenth century to the library of the abbey of Classe. It is one of only two copies of this work in Italy; there is a third copy in the Library of Congress in Washington.

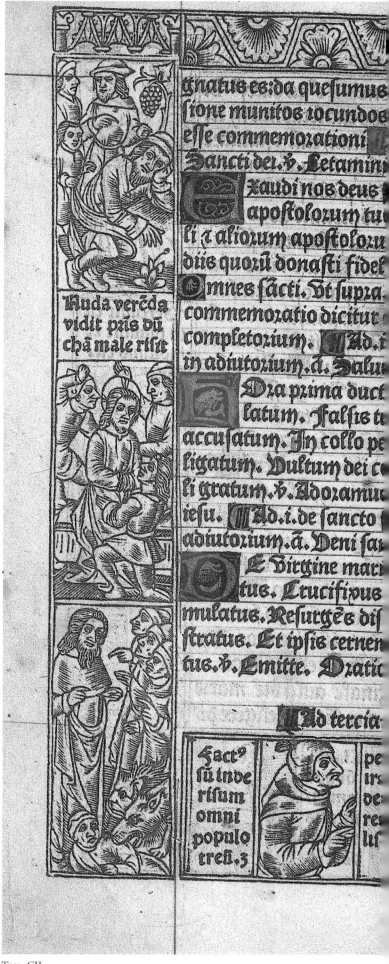

Tav. CII

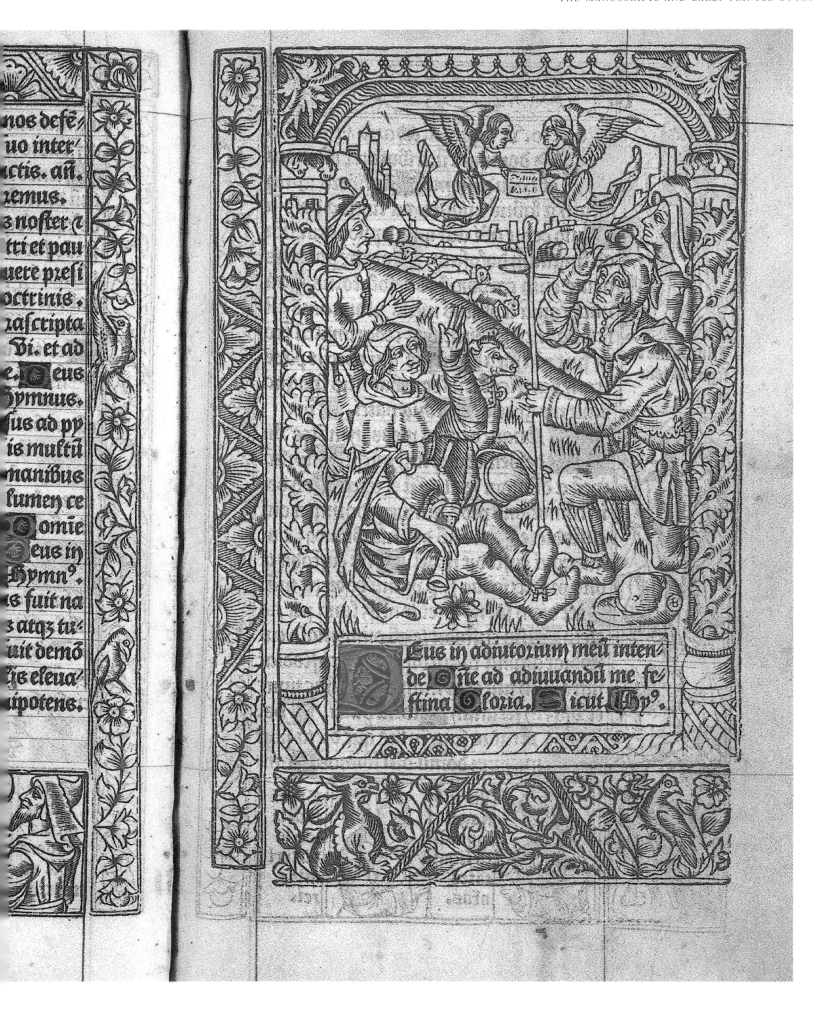

LIBER IESUS

Milan, Biblioteca Trivulziana

2163, FOL. 6

THIS SMALL CODEX (196 x 138 mm) consists of only fourteen leaves and contains short texts to be used in the education of Massimiliano Sforza, the son
of Ludovico il Moro, Duke of Milan and Beatrice d'Este, who was born in 1493.
Since it contains the alphabet, it is also known as the *Libro dell'ABC*; it includes as
well the Lord's Prayer, *Ave Maria*, Creed, Invocation of the Cross, *Miserere*, and *Salve
Regina* in Latin. These are followed by precepts and moralizing phrases, some of
which are commentaries on the miniatures. The manuscript belongs to a genre that
was fashionable in Milan and the rest of northern Italy, and which also enjoyed
success in printed editions.

The text was copied by Giovan Battista de' Lorenzi, who also wrote another fine
codex for the young Count, the *Grammar* of Donatus, as well as other Milanese
manuscripts (see pp. 230, 240, 244). The codex is decorated with numerous initials
painted on gold and blue grounds, three historiated initials, a historiated border on
fol. 3, and four full-page miniatures. Critics believe the artist of most of the scenes
representing the young Massimiliano to be Giovan Pietro Birago, a Lombard artist
influenced by both Ferrarese and Paduan art; his work is of a somewhat mediocre
quality.

The miniature of the meeting between Massimiliano Sforza and the Emperor
Maximilian, which took place at Bormio on 25 July 1496, is of much higher quality.
The young Count is depicted, accompanied by his manservant Brunoro Pietra, and
a page, as he pays homage to the Emperor Maximilian. The background shows a
wide, hilly landscape on the banks of a lake, which some scholars have identified as
Lake Como. This fine miniature is attributed to one of the finest Milanese artists
of the late fifteenth century, Boccaccio Boccaccini. He was an illuminator, but
worked mainly as a painter, and was active in Cremona from 1493 and later in Ferrara. The manuscript was probably produced between 1496 and 1498.

DONATUS, Grammar

Milan, Biblioteca Trivulziana

2167, FOLS. 42V, 1V

THIS FAMOUS SMALL CODEX was made for Massimiliano Sforza, son of Ludovico il Moro. It contains a medieval reworking of the text of Donatus, followed by a collection of moral precepts, known as the *Distica Catonis*, and the *Institutiones grammaticae*. Two sonnets are inserted at the beginning and end; the first is dedicated to Massimiliano, and the other to Ludovico il Moro.

The text was copied by Giovan Battista de' Lorenzi, a scribe who also copied the other beautiful codex for the young Sforza, the so-called *Liber Iesus*, which is also in the Biblioteca Trivulziana (see p. 238).

The decoration was executed by a number of illuminators, including Giovan Pietro Birago, an artist active at the end of the fifteenth century who decorated a large number of codices for the Sforza family, and Ambrogio de' Predis, who worked as a portrait painter at the Milanese court from 1482.

The decoration of fol. 42v, in which the young prince is represented between two female figures personifying Vice and Virtue, is attributed to Birago.

The fine portrait of Massimiliano in profile is by de' Predis, who also executed another portrait on fol. 64 of the manuscript, which is of his father Ludovico il Moro.

The codex, which is still in its original binding with the Sforza coats of arms, is datable to between 1496 and 1499.

GIOVANNI BOCCACCIO, Filostrato

Florence, Biblioteca Nazionale Centrale

PAL. E. 6. 4. III, FRONTISPIECE

THIS EDITION OF Boccaccio's *Filostrato* was printed in Milan by Ulrich Scinzenzeler in 1499 and derives from the Bolognese edition of the previous year.

Beneath the title on the frontispiece, there is a woodcut illustration representing a warrior wearing armour and a helmet; his left hand rests on a shield and in his right he holds a club. The design of the woodcut was copied from that used in Scinzenzeler's 1498 edition, which in turn is similar to that in the Bolognese edition of the same year. The woodblock for this woodcut was used again by Ulrich Scinzenzeler's son, Giovann' Angelo, for the edition of *Altobello historiato. Libro delle battaglie de li baroni di Franza*, published in Milan in 1511.

This incunable was acquired in 1829 by Grand Duke Ferdinand III de' Medici for the Palatine Library, which later passed into the National Library of Florence.

Fyloſtrato che tracta de lo inamoramento de Troylo e
Gryſeida: τ de molte altre infinite battaglie.

BOOK OF HOURS

Modena, Biblioteca Estense

LAT. 740 (= α. Q. 9. 31), FOLS. 22V, 105

ORIGINALLY THERE WAS a coat of arms surmounted by a cardinal's hat in the lower margin of the wide border which decorates the first page of the manuscript. Although this is now completely erased, it has been suggested that the manuscript, produced towards the end of the fifteenth century, belonged to Cardinal Ippolito d'Este, Archbishop of Milan in 1497.

The miniature on fol. 22v, which occupies the lower part of the page, represents a female saint, probably Saint Barbara, holding a martyr's palm, seated beside a broken column decorated on the base with an effigy of an emperor set within a medallion. On fol. 105 Mary Magdalen is shown with clasped hands and long fair hair; she stands in a building supported by four columns.

The decoration is attributable to the Lombard school of the end of the fifteenth century, and to an artist close to Francesco Binasco. The scribe of the manuscript appears to be Giovan Battista de' Lorenzi once again (see pp. 230, 238, 240).

VIRGIL, Works

Turin, Biblioteca Reale

VARIA 190, FOL. 1

THE MANUSCRIPT INCLUDES the *Bucolics*, the *Georgics* and the *Aeneid*, completed by book XIII written by the humanist Maffeo Vegio, and by other pseudo-Virgilian works. Many leaves have been removed, probably at an early date, and consequently the decorative scheme is reduced to a mere four illustrations on fols. Iv, 1, 2v and 6v.

The beginning of the *Bucolics* (fol. 1) is decorated with a wide, ornate border inhabited by seven putti in various poses. On the inner side another narrow border of fruit and laurel frames the writing space and the bucolic scene which precedes the first lines of the text. The illumination was once attributed to the Neapolitan illuminator Matteo Felice, whose activity is documented from 1467 to 1493, but who may have been active already as early as 1455, at the time when the change from late gothic features to a truly Renaissance style was first beginning. Recent scholars, however, believe that the manuscript is rather the work of Felice's workshop because of the static nature of the figures and the lack of proportion in the human bodies, particularly in the putti, whose heads are far too large in relation to their extremely short legs; they date it to the end of the fifteenth century.

The coat of arms of the person for whom the codex was made was overpainted with that of Geoffroy Carles (1460–1516), who owned the manuscript in the sixteenth century. After completing his studies in Turin, Rome and Bologna, Carles, who came from Saluzzo, held important political posts for Luigi II, the Marquis of Saluzzo, and subsequently presided over the parliament of Grenoble in 1494. He was in the retinue of Charles VIII of France in 1494 and in 1499, following the conquest of Milan, was nominated a member and later president of the Milanese Senate by Louis XII. He was in Milan from 1499 to 1512.

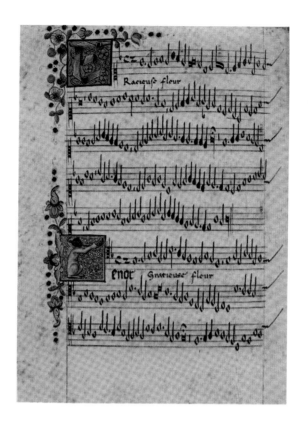

CANZONIERE FOR THREE AND FOUR VOICES

Florence, Biblioteca Nazionale Centrale

BANCO RARI 229, FOLS. 114V, IIIV

THE MANUSCRIPT IS OF PARTICULAR importance for musical studies because it is one of the most complete Song Books of the late fifteenth century; it is also illustrated by fine miniatures. The authors mainly represented are Heinrich Isaac (a Flemish composer active in Florence at the court of Lorenzo de' Medici 'il Magnifico', who later became the composer of Emperor Maximilian following the expulsion of the Medici from Florence), and Johannes Martini, a musician at the Este court in 1491; this manuscript is the most authoritative collection of his compositions. There are also other texts in French, Italian, Spanish and German; out of a total of 268 compositions, 110 are anonymous and 158 are by more or less well-known musicians.

The music, copied by a single hand, and the texts, copied in script of the late fifteenth century, are set out on 384 paper leaves decorated with borders and illuminated initials. At the beginning there are parchment flyleaves, three of which are magnificently historiated.

Fol. IIIv shown here is particularly interesting both from a decorative and musical point of view. At the centre of the page, against a uniform blue ground, is set the circular canon with the words, '*Mundus et musica et totus concentus Bartholomaeus Ramis*'. The resolution of the canon is within the circle. In the lower margin of the page, two winged putti support a cartouche inscribed, '*Omnibus hoc vitium est cantoribus inter amicos ut nunquam inducant animum cantare rogati iniussi nunquam desistant*'. This fine miniature and the two that follow are attributed to Gherardo and Monte di Giovanni.

With this manuscript the technique of fully coloured leaves is introduced to Florentine illumination; they were very rare in Florence, compared with other European centres.

VESPERAL

Verona, Biblioteca Capitolare

DCCLVIII, FOL. 109

THE MANUSCRIPT, which contains noted chants for the liturgy of Vespers, was executed in Verona towards the end of the fifteenth century. From the coat of arms on fol. iv we learn that it belonged to the Maffei family; several members of the family were canons of the Chapter.

Some of the chants are attributed to Franco-Flemish masters, but many are anonymous and are thought to have been composed by members of the school of clergy at Verona.

The decoration of the first page consists of four fine miniatures of sacred subjects: the Archangel Gabriel, the Annunciation, Saint Lucy and Saint Benedict. The following miniatures were executed by various artists, possibly by some pupils of the school; they treat a wide range of subjects.

The scene with figures on fol. 109 represents the myth of Jason killing the dragon, guardian of the Golden Fleece. The execution is lively and somewhat exaggerated, yet the design of the ships, which goes back to antique models, suggests a certain culture.

MEMOIRS OF THE FRESCHI FAMILY

Venice, Biblioteca Marciana

IT. VII. 165 (= 8867), FOL. 7

THIS MANUSCRIPT, which is datable to between the end of the fifteenth and the second half of the sixteenth century, contains the history of the Freschi family up to 1572, various documents, a book of medical prescriptions and a book of household recipes.

The text, copied by various hands, is preceded by a series of fine miniatures on the first eight pages. They depict thirteen members of the Freschi family, and with the exception of the first in the series they give the name and coat of arms of each figure.

The page shown here portrays Zaccaria Freschi, born in 1456, with his wife Dorotea. The care and attention to detail with which the clothing and hairstyles of the figures are represented can be clearly observed; for this reason these miniatures are of particular importance for the study of the dress and fashions of the time. It is possible to trace changes in style from the first identified figure, Tommaso Davide Freschi, born in 1367, to the last two, Davide Freschi and Maria Bianco, who married in 1497.

Zacarias Piscus a secretis
IIImi consilij et uxor

Dorathea Zacarias

TOURNAMENT BOOK

Vatican City, Biblioteca Apostolica Vaticana

Ross. 711, fol. 40

Tournaments, which are thought to have originated in France in the eleventh century, were originally bloody contests in which both horsemen and common people on foot participated. Although rules were introduced towards the middle of the eleventh century and blunted weapons were adopted (spears without points, unsharpened swords, harmless lances), fatal accidents often occurred. From the twelfth century the tournaments took on a more ostentatious character and were carried out following a precise ceremonial – they were preceded by a propitiatory mass and processions and were followed by feasting.

The Vatican manuscript is a fine German codex, datable to between the end of the fifteenth and the beginning of the sixteenth century, generously illustrated by drawings accompanied by brief explanations.

At the top of fol. 40 the coats of arms and names of four competitors are shown; at the bottom there is a colourful mounted horseman.

Die 4 Turnier Vögt

Mang Marschalck
von Pa pen haim
Wolff von
Waldech
Hans von
Seckendorff
Berthram von
Nesselrodt

Im Rennen, vnd Gestech
Conradt von Helmstatt, vnd Wolff von Barßberg, haben ein
gutt Rennen gethon, vnd seind baide gefallen
Es ist auch zu disem Turnier eingeritten, ein Edler Hans von Helmstatt
zu Grünbach 1481

MISSAE SUB NOTIS MUSICIS

Verona, Biblioteca Capitolare

DCCLVI, FOLS. 49, 47

THIS UNFINISHED CODEX contains the chants for three and four voices for ten masses. The chants are largely by well-known composers: Pierre de la Rue, Heinrich Isaac, Johannes Ghisalin-Verbonnet and Antoine Agricola.

The two initials shown here, a 'C' and a 'T', on brightly coloured grounds, are made up of delicate foliate motifs enlivened with flowers, fruit and small animals.

Although the original owner of the manuscript has not been identified, the most credible hypothesis is that it is linked to the Hapsburg-Burgundian court. The principal seat of the court's music chapel was at Malines, and it acquired particular importance when Philip the Fair, the son of Emperor Maximilian I, became governor of Flanders in 1494.

The manuscript is datable on stylistic grounds to the beginning of the sixteenth century. A note on fol. 1 reveals that in the eighteenth century it belonged to Francesco Bianchini, a Veronese prelate who donated it to the Biblioteca Capitolare.

BREVIARY (Grimani Breviary)

Venice, Biblioteca Marciana

LAT. I. 99 (= 2138), FOLS. 286V, 7V

T HIS CODEX CONTAINING THE LITURGY for the daily offices used by the Franciscan order consists of 832 leaves and is decorated with over one hundred full-page miniatures. The work was probably executed in the second decade of the sixteenth century, and despite differences in taste and style displays an organic whole which makes it a masterpiece of Flemish illumination.

The first pages are devoted to the calendar, with each month occupying two pages. Fol. 7v is decorated with a scene relating to the month of July set within a dark frame with late gothic features. In the foreground, sheep shearing is portrayed, while grain harvesting is shown in the field beyond the road along which a small flock of sheep is approaching. A woman spinning is seated on the threshold of a hovel and the large buildings of a town are seen in the background.

Following the calendar sixty-eight illustrations have been inserted in the text, taken from the Old and New Testaments and from the lives of the saints. The scenes are set beside historiated and decorated initials, and monochrome borders with architectural frames alternate with others decorated with flowers, foliate motifs and small animals.

There is no documentation on the commissioning or preparation of the manuscript. It is attributed to a workshop influenced by the most important centres of Flemish illumination, Bruges and Ghent. It was illuminated by Gerard Horenbout (who probably executed the whole of the calendar), Alexander Bening, his son Simon, and other minor assistants.

In 1520, as soon as it was completed the Breviary was sold by Antonio Siciliano, chamberlain of Massimiliano Sforza and ambassador to Flanders, to Cardinal Domenico Grimani (1461–1523), a humanist and collector. The manuscript is still linked to the Cardinal's name and has become famous as the Grimani Breviary.

RAFFAELE BRANDOLINI LIPPO,
De laudibus eloquentiae

Ravenna, Biblioteca Classense

39, FOLS. 4, 1

R AFFAELE BRANDOLINI, an Augustinian priest, dedicated his life more to study than to the Church. He was educated in Naples, at the Accademia del Pontano, taught rhetoric and became a renowned composer of Latin prose and extemporary verse and these achievements gained him the favour of Pope Leo X (Giovanni de' Medici, son of Lorenzo 'il Magnifico'). The present work, which is dedicated to Leo X, is a sermon that Brandolini gave at the church of San Eustachio in Rome on 18 October 1513, praising the plan for the reform of studies promoted by the Pope.

This small manuscript must be the copy that Brandolini presented to the Pope. It has a letter of dedication (fol. 4) and the Medici coat of arms and family devices (a diamond ring with the motto 'SEMPER', the three feathers and the bough (*broncone*), as well as Leo's personal device of the yoke) appear in the decoration of the frontispiece on fol. 1. The two pages are very fully decorated: not only are there decorated borders and initials, but the headings are written in gold on painted coloured grounds.

The artist who executed the decoration cannot be identified with any major illuminator, but he may have been a pupil of the famous Florentine illuminator Attavante, who clearly influenced his style.

RAPHAEL BRANDO
LINVS IVNIOR
LIPPVS LEONI
X PONT OPT
MAX SALVTEM
A C
FOELICITATE
D

NVITANT
ne quotidie ad lu
cubrandum ac di
cendum maxime
uae clarissimae q, et priuatae et
publicae actiones Nihil enim

PIER CATTACI, Medici genealogy

Florence, Biblioteca Medicea Laurenziana

MED. PAL. 225, FOL. 1

T HIS MANUSCRIPT, which consists of ten leaves containing the genealogy of the Medici family, was compiled by Pier Cattaci for Pope Leo X, who in lay life had been Giovanni de' Medici, the son of Lorenzo 'il Magnifico'. On fol. 2, preceding the genealogical tree painted on the following pages, are a dedicatory letter to the Pope, and the coat of arms of Leo X painted between two lesser coats: those of Lorenzo, Duke of Urbino, and of Madeleine de la Tour d'Auvergne. It is probable that the manuscript was given to the Pope on the occasion of the marriage of Lorenzo to Madeleine in 1518, or immediately afterwards.

Although the illumination of these pages is of somewhat mediocre quality, the decoration of the first page of the manuscript is of a quite different order. It is occupied by a true painting, showing Saints Cosmas and Damian, the patron saints of the Medici family. The painting is attributed to Francesco Ubertini, known as 'il Bachiacca' (1494–1557), a Florentine painter, who was particularly talented in executing works in small dimensions. On grounds of style and in comparison with other works this painting can be dated to 1524 or 1525, after the death of Leo X.

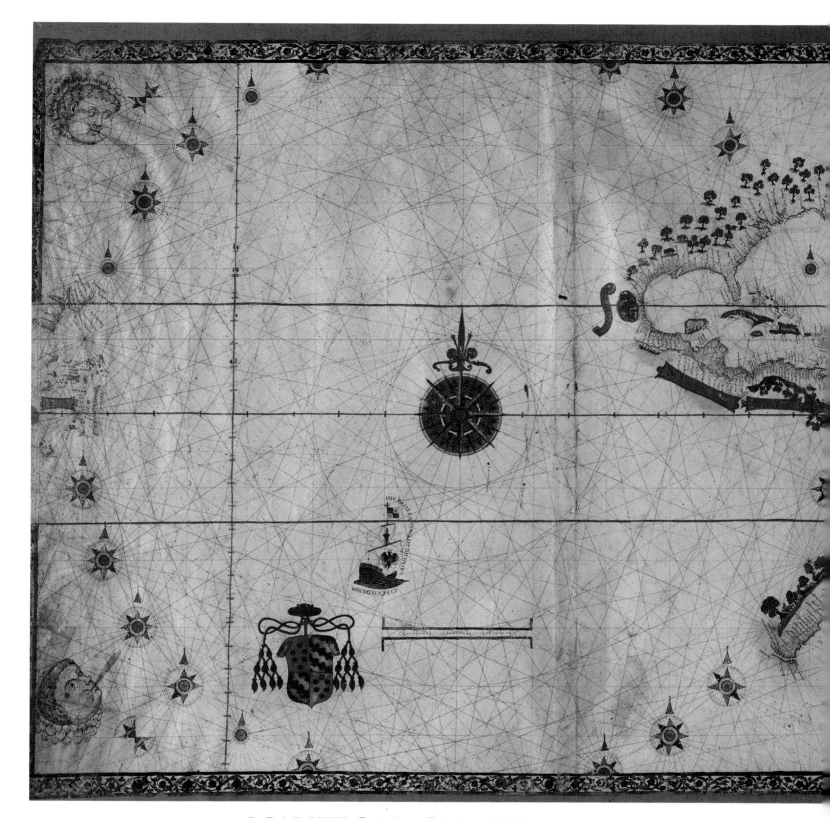

NAUTICAL CHART

Florence, Biblioteca Medicea Laurenziana

MED. PAL. 249

THIS LARGE NAUTICAL CHART, on parchment and measuring approximately one metre in width by two metres in length, is very accurately drawn. It can be dated to about 1525 and was produced by a Catalan cartographer for Cardinal Giovanni Salviati (whose coat of arms appears twice). Salviati was Papal Nunzio in Spain and was given the chart by the Emperor Charles V. The map shows the whole world as it was then known, from India to the East coast of America.

PSALTER

Ravenna, Biblioteca Classense

600, FOLS. 78, 123V

T HIS PSALTER IN TWO VOLUMES (MSS. 600 and 597) was made for the monastery of Santa Maria in Porto in Ravenna. The decoration of the manuscript consists of numerous initials of various types, and six pages with historiated initials and borders filling the four margins. The monastery's coat of arms is included in the lower borders of all but one of these pages.

Although the six pages were written by the same scribe as the rest of the Psalter, they are distinguished from the body of the manuscript because they were decorated by a different artist, Giovanni Battista Cavalletto. His style is characterized by figures with either youthful faces or white beards, drapery incised in sharp folds and barely sketched backgrounds. The borders with foliate motifs surrounding the pages and the initials enclosing the figures show a marked tendency to stylization. Recent scholarship has dated the execution of the manuscript to the end of the 1520s when Cavalletto was in Rome.

The figures in the minor initials (fol. 78 shows Bishop Atanasio) appear to be by Scipione Cavalletto, Giovanni Battista's son, who painted fuller faces and softer drapery.

PIETRO APIANO, Astronomicum caesareum

Florence, Biblioteca Nazionale Centrale

MAGL. 5. 41, FOLS. 27V-28

Pietro apiano was born in 1495 in Saxony, studied at Leipzig University and soon became known as a talented mathematician and astronomer. He taught at Ingolstadt University, where he remained until his death in 1551. The *Astronomicum caesareum*, dedicated to Emperor Charles V, was published in 1540. It contains numerous drawings, paintings, diagrams and tables, many of which have movable parts for the study of planets.

In this work, the author proposes the substitution of instruments, with which it would be possible to trace the position of the stars and of eclipses, for the old astronomical tables. He also describes an instrument, the *torquetum*, which helped to solve astronomical triangulations, and completes the work with observations on the comets of 1531, 1532, 1533, 1538 and 1539.

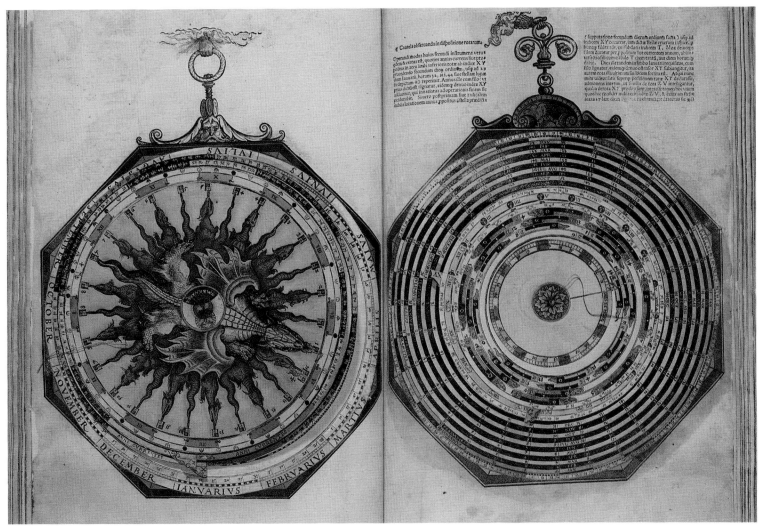

PIER ANTONIO MICHIEL, Herbal

Venice, Biblioteca Marciana

IT. II. 29 (= 4863), VOL. IV, FOL. 87

THIS MANUSCRIPT is the autograph of Pier Antonio Michiel, a Venetian patrician who lived between 1510 and 1576. His imposing botanical treatise describing over one thousand plants is divided into five volumes, which each have their own page numbering and are distinguished by the parchment bindings: red for volumes I and II, green for volume III, yellow for volume IV and violet blue for volume V.

On the recto of each leaf there is a watercolour drawing of a plant, executed with extreme refinement and attention to detail by the painter Domenico dalle Greche. On the verso are the vernacular name and a description of the plant, accompanied by interesting physiological observations, which often anticipate the studies of other botanists, and a rich lexicon of the regional names of the various species.

The painting shown here is taken from the fourth volume, the 'yellow book'.

In the eighteenth century the manuscript belonged to G. A. Bonato, Professor of Botany at the University of Padua, who donated it to the Biblioteca Marciana.

The first edition of Michiel's work was printed in 1940 with the title, *I cinque libri di piante.*

CRISTOFORO CANAL, Della militia maritima
(On the maritime militia)

Venice, Biblioteca Marciana

IT. IV. 50 (= 5544), FOL. 96

CRISTOFORO CANAL, who came from an aristocratic Venetian family, embarked upon a maritime career and made substantial changes to Venetian military organization. He maintained the necessity of using forced ship's crews, who had to be treated humanely since there were few volunteer oarsmen available. His idea, which was supported by the government which appointed him 'Governor of convicts', made it possible for him to arm six galleys between 1545 and 1547. In 1558 he was appointed general superintendent, the highest appointment in the fleet in peace time. He took part personally in several battles; in 1560 he captured the Genoese pirate Filippo Cicala and in 1562 he defeated a fleet of pirates off Corfù. Besides being an expert seaman, he was also a cultivated and studious man; in 1560 he wrote *Della militia maritima*, a treatise on marine administration and naval techniques.

On fol. 96 of the Biblioteca Marciana manuscript is shown Canal's ideal galley, which he described thus: 'The perfect galley should be like a fair maiden, showing readiness and vivacity in all her gestures; she should be agile, but not so much so that she lacks appropriate dignity'.

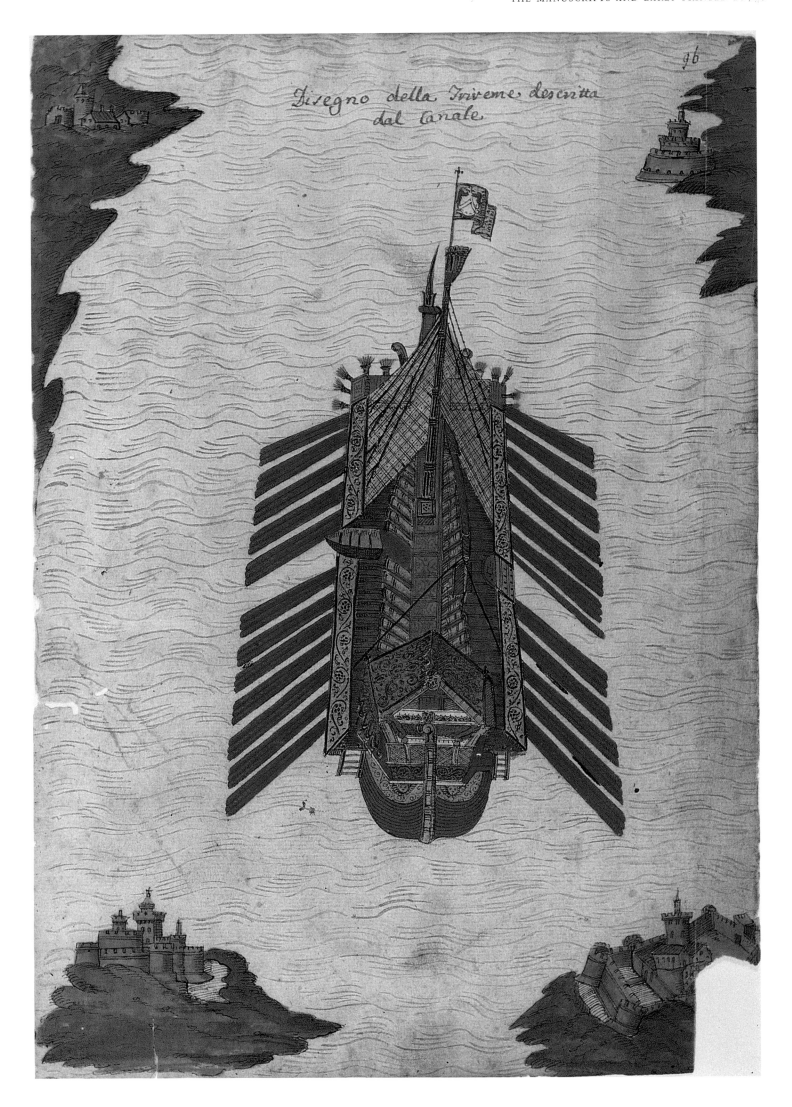

Disegno della Triveme descritta
dal Canale

GIACOMO MAGGIOLO, Nautical chart of the Mediterranean

Rome, Biblioteca Casanatense

4865

THIS NAUTICAL CHART of the Mediterranean is in the form of a parchment roll (920 x 780 mm). We learn from its colophon that it was executed by Giacomo Maggiolo in Genoa in 1558.

The chart is extremely accurate, both in its outline of the coast and islands and indication of place names, and in its decoration, which is by an artist who was refined and precise in his depiction of cities, peoples and rulers.

Two details are particularly noteworthy. Firstly, the representation in the left margin of three sailing ships, which probably refer to the voyage of Christopher Columbus, and secondly, the representation of Genoa and Venice, whose commercial importance the artist probably wished to underline.

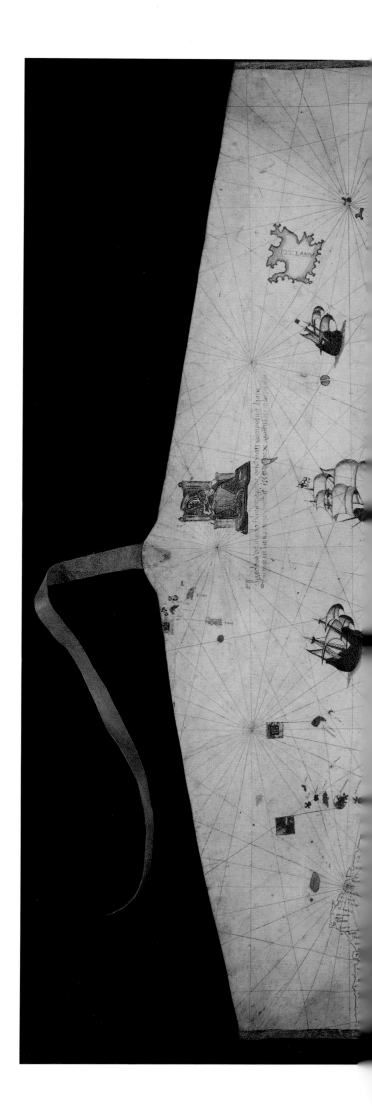

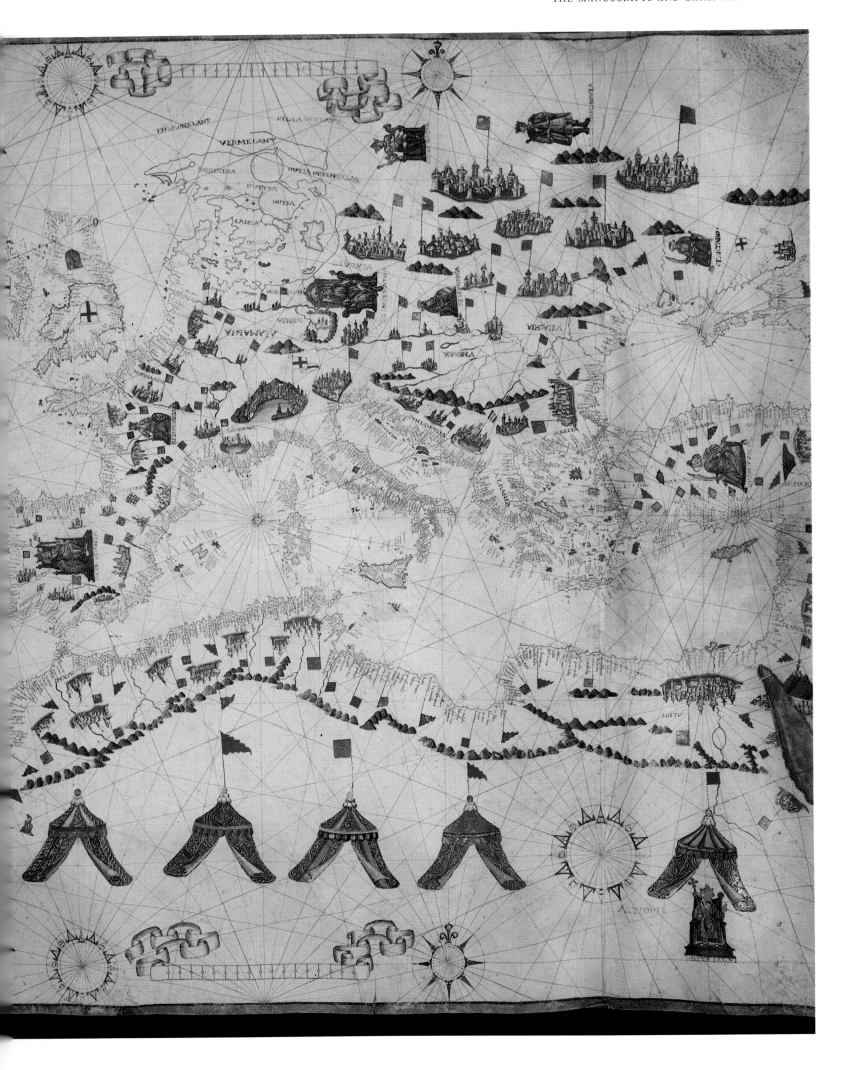

LEO VI, Oracles

Palermo, Biblioteca Centrale

I. E. 8, FOLS. 4, 2

THIS MANUSCRIPT IS IN GREEK and contains fifteen prophecies of the Emperor Leo VI the Wise (886–912) concerning the end of the Comnenian empire and the conquest of Constantinople by the Turks.

The text takes up fifteen pages, each of which is illustrated with a miniature accompanied by verses. The drawings, outlined in pen and later coloured, are of Byzantine derivation, but were probably executed in Sicily as there are both eastern and western elements in them.

The fourth Oracle is shown on fol. 4. There is a city wall with two gates, one open, the other closed; on the walls are four towers, three have domed roofs and one a conical roof. At the bottom, to the left, a goblet containing a severed head is linked to the walls by a rivulet of blood.

The miniature on fol. 2 illustrates the second Oracle: there is a unicorn with a quarter moon on its right hind flank. At the bottom is a small male figure.

The manuscript belonged to the Jesuit Collegio Massimo in Palermo and is thought to have been produced between 1566 and 1574, during the reign of the Ottoman Sultan Selim II.

BERNARDO BUONTALENTI,
Sketches for the costumes for the Intermezzi of 1589

Florence, Biblioteca Nazionale Centrale

PAL. C. B. 3. 53, VOL. II, FOLS. 29, 30V-31

BERNARDO BUONTALENTI (1536–1608) was one of the most active Florentine Mannerist architects and also worked as a sculptor. He drew up the plans for the town of Livorno and created scenery for feasts and spectacles. To mark the marriage of Ferdinando I de' Medici to Cristina of Lorraine in 1589, he designed the scenery, costumes, ornaments and chariots for the six *Intermezzi* (Intervals) in Gerolamo Bargagli's play, *Pellegrina.*

The sketches shown here, executed on coarse paper, are outlined in pen and painted in watercolour. The scene on fol. 29 is for the first *Intermezzo.* Four gods are shown: Mercury, Apollo, Jupiter and Asteria. On fols. 30v–31 the Hamadryad nymphs are shown on the slopes of a steep hill. According to the plan shown in the sketch, the nymphs entered the stage on an engine that was seven metres in height, greatly amazing the spectators.

JAN VAN DER STRAET,
Collection of drawings

Florence, Biblioteca Medicea Laurenziana

MED. PAL. 75, FOL. 51

THE FLEMING JAN VAN DER STRAET (1523–1606) was known in Italy as Giovanni Stradano. He was a painter and designer of cartoons for tapestries and of drawings for engravings and decorative works, and spent most of his career in Florence at the courts of Cosimo I and Francesco I de' Medici.

The present manuscript contains numerous drawings illustrating the *Divine Comedy* and five concerning the discovery of America. Four of the latter, illustrating the voyages of Christopher Columbus, Amerigo Vespucci and Ferdinand Magellan, were the preparatory drawings for the prints which were to illustrate Adriaen Collaert's work, *Americae Retectio*, printed by Philippe Galle.

The picture reproduced here shows Amerigo Vespucci standing on board a ship as it approaches the American coast. The inscription on the mast, 'IOANNI / STRAD / ANUS / INVEN / 1589 / ESCUD', dates the work to 1589. It is probable that these drawings were sent to Antwerp in the same year or shortly afterwards to be used in the printed edition: there are instructions to the engraver in the upper margins.

INSIGNA FAMILIARUM (Archinto)

Turin, Biblioteca Reale

ST. IT. 138, FOLS. 3V, 4

THIS ANONYMOUS WORK contains a collection of coats of arms mainly of Lombard families. It is probable that the work, in two volumes, belonged to Count Ottavio Archinto, a patron and historian, and indeed the manuscript is generally known by his name, 'Archinto'.

The first volume opens with the coats of arms of Pope Pius IV (1550–1565), the Emperor and the kings of Spain and France. These are followed by a figure of a woman (fol. 3v). Her dress is decorated with the coat of arms of the Visconti family and she holds two crested helmets; this is the first of a series of sixty Visconti coats of arms and devices (see fol. 4). The coats of arms of the principal rulers of Europe and Asia, as well as of noble families (in part left incomplete) are also included.

The second volume opens with the coat of arms of Pope Paul V (1566–1572).

Although the manuscript has little value from an artistic point of view, it is extremely important as a repertory of heraldry.

¶ Arma nobilissimi Vicecomitis
dñi dñi mediolani et comitis
anglie ab antico et vicary
inpeualis :

¶ Azo Viccecomes dñi domini
mediolani :

Dñs dñs Archieps Johanes Vicecomes dñi mediolani
et Janue et florentie et cetera.

Dñs luchinus Vicecomes dñs mediolani et comes
anglie.

SELECT BIBLIOGRAPHY

Alexander, J.J.G., *Italian Renaissance Illumination*, London and New York 1977
——, *Medieval Illuminators and their Methods of Work*, New Haven and London 1992
Armstrong, L., *Renaissance Miniature Painting and Classical Imagery*, London 1981
Avril, F. and Reynaud N., *Les manuscrits à peintures en France 1440–1520*, Paris 1994
Berg, K., *Studies in Tuscan Twelfth-century Illumination*, Oslo 1968
Biblioteca Apostolica Vaticana, Florence 1985
Biblioteca Capitolare, Verona, Florence 1994
Biblioteca Casanatense, Roma, Florence 1993
Biblioteca Centrale della Regione Siciliana, Palermo, Florence 1992
Biblioteca Classense, Ravenna, Florence 1996
Biblioteca Estense, Modena, Florence 1987
Biblioteca Marciana, Venezia, Florence 1988
Biblioteca Medicea Laurenziana, Firenze, Florence 1986
Biblioteca Nazionale Napoli, Florence 1993
Biblioteca Nazionale Centrale, Firenze, Florence 1989
Biblioteca Reale, Torino, Florence 1990
Biblioteca Trivulziana, Milano, Florence 1995
Biblioteche d'Italia. Le biblioteche pubbliche statali, Rome 1991
Brown, M.P., *Understanding Illuminated Manuscripts. A Guide to Technical Terms*, J. Paul Getty Museum and British Library 1994
Le Collezioni d'arte della Biblioteca Reale di Torino. Disegni, incisioni, manoscritti figurati, G.C. Scrolla (ed.), Turin 1985
Conti, A., *La miniatura bolognese. Scuole e botteghe 1270–1340*, Bologna 1981
I Corali del Monastero di Santa Maria degli Angeli e le loro miniature asportate, M. Levi D'Ancona, A. Dillon Bussi, A.R. Fantoni, D. Savelli (eds), exhib. cat., Florence 1995

D'Ancona, P., *La miniatura fiorentina (secc. XI–XVI)*, 2 vols, Florence 1914
D'Ancona, P. and Aeschlimann, E., *The Art of Illumination. An Anthology of Manuscripts from the Sixth to the Sixteenth Century*, London 1969
Daneu Lattanzi, A., *I manoscritti ed incunaboli miniati della Sicilia*, vol. 1: *Biblioteca Nazionale di Palermo*, Rome 1965
De Hamel, C., *Scribes and Illuminators*, London 1992
——, *A History of Illuminated Manuscripts*, 2nd edn, London 1994
Dillon Bussi, A., *Miniature laurenziane rinascimentali. Nuove proposte attributive*, Florence 1991
Diringer, D., *The Illuminated Book. Its History and Production*, London 1958
Dogaer, G., *Flemish Miniature Painting in the Fifteenth and Sixteenth Centuries*, Amsterdam 1987
Fava, D. and Salmi, M., *I manoscritti miniati della Biblioteca Estense di Modena*, vols I–II, Florence 1950–73
Garzelli, A., *La Bibbia di Federico da Montefeltro. Un'officina libraria fiorentina 1476–1478*, Rome 1977
Harthan, J., *Books of Hours and their Owners*, London 1977
Hermann, J.H., *La miniatura estense*, F. Toniolo (ed.), Modena 1994
Limentani Virdis, C., *Codici miniati fiamminghi e olandesi nelle biblioteche dell'Italia nord-orientale*, Vicenza 1981
I luoghi della memoria scritta. Manoscritti, incunaboli, libri a stampa di Biblioteche Statali Italiane, exhib. cat., Rome 1994

Mariani Canova, G., *La miniatura veneta del Rinascimento*, Venice 1968
Miniatura fiorentina del Rinascimento 1440–1525. Un primo censimento, A. Garzelli (ed.), 2 vols, Florence 1985
Miniature del Rinascimento, exhib. cat. for the quincentenary of the Biblioteca Vaticana, Vatican 1950
Morello, G., *Libri d'ore della Biblioteca Apostolica Vaticana*, Zurich 1988
Mostra storica nazionale della miniatura, exhib. cat., Florence 1953
Le Muse e il Principe. Arte di corte nel Rinascimento italiano, exhib. cat., 2 vols, Modena 1991
Pächt, O., *Book Illumination in the Middle Ages: An Introduction*, London 1986
The Painted Page. Italian Renaissance Book Illumination 1450–1550, J.J.G. Alexander (ed.), exhib. cat., London 1994
Piazzi, A., *La più antica biblioteca d'Europa: la Capitolare di Verona*, Verona 1986
Porcher, J., *French Miniatures from Illuminated Manuscripts*, London, 1960
Pregare nel segreto. Libri d'Ore e testi di spiritualità nella tradizione cristiana, G. Cavallo (academic adviser), B. Tellini Santoni and A. Manodori (co-ordinators), exhib. cat., Rome 1994
Raffaello e la Roma dei papi, G. Morello (ed.), exhib. cat., Rome 1986
Salmi, M., *Italian Miniatures*, New York 1957
Santoro, C., *I tesori della Trivulziana*, Milan 1962
Toesca, P., *La pittura e la miniatura in Lombardia dai più antichi monumenti alla metà del Quattrocento*, Milan 1932
Vedere i classici. L'illustrazione libraria dei testi antichi dall'età romana al tardo Medioevo, M. Buonocore (ed.), exhib. cat., Rome 1996

LIST OF MANUSCRIPTS
AND PRINTED BOOKS

arranged chronologically by library